RAILWAYS REVISITED

A Guide to little-known railways in AUSTRIA and GERMANY

Credit for photos in this book are to be found in parentheses at the end of each photo caption.

Cover photos, clockwise from top left.

Albtalbahn; (photo by Bernhardt Hoch)

Zugspitzbahn; (BZB photo by Huber)

Fribourg Funicular;

RAILWAYS REVISITED

A guide to little-known
railways in
AUSTRIA and GERMANY

By Bernard C. Winn

First printing

INCLINE PRESS---MERCED, CA 95340

To Audrey

RAILWAYS   REVISITED
A guide to little-known railways
in AUSTRIA and GERMANY

By Bernard C. Winn

Published by:

 Incline Press
456 Columbia Ave.
P.O.Box 212
Merced, CA 95340

First Printing 1988
Printed in the United States of America

Library of Congress Catalog Card number: 87-83256
ISBN 0-9615161-1-9

TABLE OF CONTENTS

PREFACE

This book is intended both as a guide and as an introduction to some of Austria's and Germany's most unusual and interesting railways. Although there are a great many railways within these two countries, only cable (funicular), rack and pinion, and steam railways will be dealt with here.

As is the case with many other attractions, the least-known are often the most rewarding. It is with that thought in mind that this book has been written. Only a very few of the railways described in this book will be found in any of the best-selling travel guides.

It is especially hoped that railway enthusiasts will find this work informative enough to be of some help in the pursuit of their interest in the subject. For additional or more technical information about any particular railway, however, one should either write to the company or try to visit the railway itself.

Funiculars and rack railways although plentiful in Europe, are all but unknown on this side of the Atlantic; there being only two rack lines and probably less than a dozen funiculars in the entire United States. Steam railways, on the other hand, seem to be popular world-wide and nowhere are they more prevelant than in Austria and Germany.

Great effort has been made to ensure the accuracy of the information contained in this book. However, since much of the information was contributed by the railways involved, neither the author nor the publisher can accept any resonsibility for errors, omissions, or changes unknown to them at the time of publication. HAPPY TRAVELING.

CHAPTER ONE

INTRODUCTION
TO FUNICULAR AND RACK RAILWAYS

Since, as stated earlier, these types of railways are nearly unknown in our country, the following descriptions and explanations are offered.

FUNICULARS

Most funicular railways operate on the principle of counterbalancing an ascending car with a descending one. To accomplish this, two passenger cars are attached to opposite ends of a long cable that has been passed over a pulley and around a winding mechanism at the top of an incline. Further, to make the thing function, it is considered necessary to add a power source either to the cars themselves, or to the lifting mechanism, or both.

Most early-day funiculars were of the "water balance" or "hydraulic" type. The two cars ascended and descended an incline using only gravitational force, and a volume of water for counterbalancing one car with another; no conventional power source was used or needed.

To set the funicular into motion, water was introduced into the tank of the car at the top of the hill (a large tank was carried under each car). Once filled, the weight of the car was such that, when the braking mechanism was released, the car would descend. The descending car, with its extra weight, also acted as a counter-balance to lift the "bottom" car to the top. When the transfer was completed, the water was released from the bottom car and the whole process repeated.

Except for the water balance funiculars in

Early-day "water balance" funicular.

Fribourg Switzerland and Wiesbaden Germany, practically all European funiculars are operated by electricity, the power usually being applied to a motor at the top station.

The length of the cable used on a funicular railway is equal to the length of the track, plus the turns on the winding drums of the lifting mechanism. As a result, when one car is at the top, the other will be at the bottom and when they are at the half-way point, they will be side by side.

The normal layout of a funicular line consists of a single set of tracks from top to bottom with a small section of double track, called a "loop," at the half-way point to allow the cars to pass each other. There are three or four other track configurations, but the above arrangement is by far the most common.

To avoid a complicated switching system, only the wheels that ride the outside rail have flanges. The flanges have the effect of forcing the car onto the loop and then back to the main line after the cars have passed each other. One car always goes to the right and the other to the left.

The size of funiculars, and it varies a great deal, is usually determined by the needs of the particular location. There are some that will barely hold 20 people, while others can comfortably carry 200 or more. In the winter resort areas, it is not uncommon to see two large cars operating in tandem to handle the extra traffic.

There are three distinct types of cars used by funicular railways: stepped; wedge-tram; and tram.

The most common of these is the stepped type which is so named because it is built as a series of separate compartments, each a step above the next. Most of them are finished off with a common roof for all compartments, which has the effect of making the cars look like a parallagram-shaped box on wheels. The stepped cars that don't have the continuous roof configuration look very much like a flight of stairs on wheels. Either way, they are unusual looking and take some getting used to. At the stations, the cars are often entered or exited via a staircase that serves as a platform alongside the inclined tracks. Usually, but not always, each compartment has a door to the outside and passengers can move freely from one compartment to another. On some of the stepped cars, however, especially those used on steep inclines, there is so much difference between the floor levels of the compartments, passage from one to the other is not practical.

A "stepped" type funicular without the continuous-roof configuration for all compartments.

The <u>wedge-tram</u> style car consists of a regular tram car mounted on a wedge shaped rail car. The point of the wedge faces up the incline and supports the car in a horizontal position. When in the station, the wedge is out of sight and the car looks quite normal. When viewed from the down side as it leaves or approaches the station, however, it easily qualifies as one of the homeliest vehicles ever built.

The wedge-shaped rail car was developed many years ago and was intended only to carry freight and horse carriages up and down hills too steep for the horses to climb. The passenger car was an afterthought and certainly looks like it.

The <u>tram</u> style cars--with no stepped compartments and no ugly wedge--are the only normal looking ones of the lot. Unfortunately, they lack the comfort of the other cars on steep inclines due to having the floor and seats on a plane parallel to the tracks, rather than the horizontal. On the other hand, they are seldom found on steep routes, so it is of minor importance.

There is another type of cable railway in Europe known as an <u>Inclined Cable Lift</u> or Schragaufzug (Ger.). It's appearance is similar to the predecessor of the wedge-tram type funicular and for the same reason. They were built primarily for hauling equipment and supplies, rather than for passengers. In place of the usual car of some kind in which to sit, they have only a bare platform. Supported by a wedge-shaped car and riding on widely separated tracks, it is raised and lowered by a cable hoist situated at the top of the incline. Because they generally have only one car, a single set of tracks, without a loop, is usually sufficient.

Because incline cable lifts fit the dictionary's rather vague definition of a funicular and, at least for the sake of statistics, they are called funiculars, they will be considered as such in this book.

The six inclined cable lifts described in this book are all located in the Kaprun Valley of Austria and include the world's largest cable railway and Europe's steepest cable railway.

It will be noticed that the steepness of the routes of funiculars in particular, and trains in general, is expressed as <u>percent gradient</u>. Although this is common practice, it's none-the-less confusing to the uninitiated. A gradient of 85%, for instance, does not mean you are going to be traveling nearly vertically up or down. The ambiguity lies in the fact that it is easy to confuse percent with degree. A 47% gradient, for example, represents an incline of only 21.1 degrees. To find the true angle of travel, you must apply a formula for solving a right triangle. <u>The sine of the angle of travel being equal to the difference of altitude, divided by the distance traveled.</u>

Example: If you gain 360 feet in altitude over a route that is 1000 feet in length, the gradient is stated as being 47%. Dividing 360 (the diff. in alt.), by 1000 (the distance traveled), you get .36000, which is the sine of a 21.1 degree angle. Therefore, your true rate of ascent/descent, is 21.1 degrees. To find the gradient, you just multiply the angle by 1/45, in this case the answer is of course 47%. Steepness is also sometimes expresed in terms of ratios. For example, it might be said that an incline is one in four, or one in five, etc. For the sake of simplicity, the ratio is generally arrived at by dividing the gradient into 100%. Example: A 25% gradient, divided into 100%, gives you a ratio of 1 in 4; a gradient of 45% divided into 100% gives you a ratio of 1 in 2.2; etc.

Although funiculars operate at gradients upwards of 100%, they have enviable safety records, due in part to the presence of multiple braking systems. Also, one of the functions of the operator of the car is to observe the condition of the cable that supports the car. The cables ordinarily last for several years but they do require maintainance and frequent inspection to insure their safeness.

For the purpose of this book, funiculars may also be referred to as cable railways or cable cars.

RACK/COG RAILWAYS

Swiss engineer Riggenbach perfected the rack and pinion system for railways in 1869 and used it for the first time in 1871 on the Vitnau-Rigi Railway, which is still in service today.

Rack railways differ from ordinary railways in that they are equipped with a mechanism that enables them to ascend gradients beyond the ability of adhesion alone. Many rack lines use a combination of rack and adhesion, engaging the rack only when necessary.

The rack is a ladder arrangement, or a row of steel teeth in some configuration, fastened securely in the center between the rails in a position parallel to, but usually slightly higher than, the rails. When engaged by a powered pinion or cogwheel, the car "climbs the rack" and with no possibility of slipping backwards. When descending, the power to the pinion is reversed and the engine becomes a generator, and the rack and pinion provide added braking power.

There are four types of racks used on European railways: Riggenbach; Abt; Strub; and Locher.

The <u>Riggenbach rack</u>, which looks like a steel ladder with closely spaced rungs, is limited to gradients of approximately 25%, or a ratio of 1 in 4. This was the first type of rack used and it can still be found on some old funiculars, as they were originally used for added braking power. There are, of course, several rack railways that still use this type of system.

The Abt rack and pinion system, showing the two rows of staggered teeth.

The <u>Abt rack</u> uses two parallel rows of teeth set on edge and staggered in pitch which are meshed with two corresponding rows of teeth on the car's pinion wheel. This system has also been widely used as a source of braking power on funicular railways.

The <u>Strub rack</u> is similar to the above, except that, instead of the two rows of staggered teeth, it has only one row of large teeth.

The <u>Locher System</u> was developed especially for the Pilatus Railway which has a maximum gradient of 48%. It uses two horizontal driving cogwheels that rotate about vertical shafts in a plane parallel to the rails, their teeth engaging sideways with teeth cut horizontally into each side of the rack. Flat rotary disks under the driving pinions have flanges that run on each side of the rack below the teeth and help to guide the car and prevent it from lifting off the tracks.

Rack railways are truly mountain railways and their use comes into play where adhesion lines leave off, which is when the gradient becomes greater than 7.3%. Rack lines also have a gradient limit, which at the present time is considered to be 48%. Funiculars on the other hand can ascend gradients in excess of 100%.

One might think that funiculars could replace rack railways and maybe even some adhesion lines since they can operate over such a wide range of gradients. The problem with that idea is that the weight of the cable for the funiculars is such that it limits the length of funicular railways to just over two miles in length. If the distance to be covered is greater than that, another separate line has to be built and passengers must change cars to

The Strub rack of the Schneebergbahn, with its single row of large teeth. (O.B.B.).

continue on. There are a few two stage funicular lines in existance and at one time there was even a three stage one, but they are neither practical nor popular.

Many funiculars have been replaced by aerial cableways which are cheaper to build and maintain. In Austria however, just the opposite has been occuring lately. There they have been building some very large and fast funiculars, to replace some of their aerial cablecars. The secret to their success is in the use of tunnels and trestles to protect the route from avalanches, thereby making them safe and useable during the winter. Although funiculars are more expensive initially, they can carry more passengers for less money than can aerial trams. Until recently, however, winter weather conditions often limited their usefulness during the busiest part of the year.

Aerial view, showing the elevated tracks of the 7708 foot Hart-kaiserbahn as they extend from the base station, at bottom right, to the 5085 foot summit of the Hartkaiser. (Studio P. St Johann i.T.).

The elevated tracks of the Olympiabahn at Axamer Lizum, site of the 1964 and 1976 Olympics. (Tourist Office, Axams/tirol).

A U S T R I A N
FUNICULAR AND RACK RAILWAYS

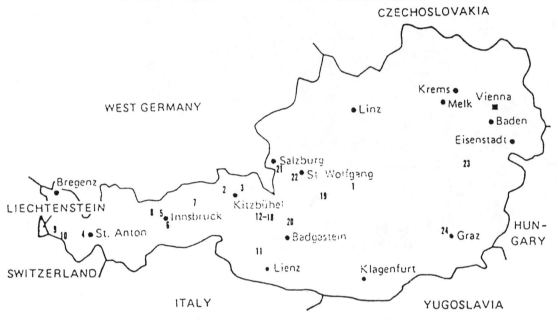

1	WURZERALM-SEILBAHN	13	GLETSCHERBAHN KAPRUN 2
2	HARTKAISERBAHN	14	SCHRAGAUFZUG LIMBERSTOLLEN
3	BERGBAHNEN ST. JOHANN	15	SCHRAGAUFZUG LIMBER WEST
4	ALBERGER BERGBAHNEN	16	SCHRAGAUFZUG LIMBER EAST
5	HUNGERBURGBAHN	17	SCHRAGAUFZUG MOLLPUMPWERK
6	OLYMPIABAHN	18	LARCHWANDAUFZUG
7	ACHENSEEBAHN	19	SALZBERGBAHN
8	SEILBAHN SEEFELD-TIROL	20	SCHLOSSALM STANDSEILBAHN
9	GOLMERBAHN	21	FESTUNGBAHN
10	VERMUNTBAHN	22	SCHRAFBERG-RAILWAY
11	GROSSGLOCKNER GLETSCHERBAHN	23	SCHNEEBERG-BAHN
12	MAISKOGEL-SCHRAGAUFZUG	24	GRAZER SCHLOSSBERGBAHN

CHAPTER TWO

AUSTRIAN
FUNICULAR AND RACK RAILWAYS

With a large number of funiculars, three rack railways and about two dozen tourist steam railways, Austria rivals Switzerland when it comes to the number and variety of its railways.

Just as in Switzerland, nearly all of Austria's funiculars are located in the winter resort areas and include some of the longest ones in Europe.

WURZERALMBAHN

A modern car of the 1.88 mile Wurzeralmbahn avoiding the winter's snow. (Voest-Alpine AG).

The Wurzeralmbahn, constructed in 1978, is one of a new breed of large and fast, all weather funiculars that have appeared on the scene since 1969. The aluminum cars carry 140 passengers in six separate compartments, each of which has four automatically controlled doors to enable quick on and off boarding.

At 1.88 miles long, the Wurzeralmbahn is one of the longest single-section funicular railways in Europe. All but 2300 feet of its tracks are carried on concrete trusses above the ground, the other 2300 feet being contained in 3 tunnels near the top of the run. The raised tracks and the tunnels help protect the railway from avalanches.

The average gradient is only 21.5 %, with a maximum of 30%, but the cars lift you 2023 feet up the mountain slope to the upper station and restaurant in only 6 minutes, a very fast ride for a cable railway.

With tinted windows, nicely upholstered seats and special shock absorbers, the cars have been designed to provide a comfortable and pleasant trip under all weather conditions.

Funiculars, having safe, positive and reliable braking systems, are the safest cable drawn conveyances in existance and these new ones are state of the art. Unlike most of the systems, this one has its lifting mechanism under the platform of the lower station, which has some definite advantages when it comes to service and repair during the winter months.

The lower station of the Wurzeralmbahn is located a short distance west of the town of Spital/Pyhrn and operation is from 0830 until 1630 daily.

Five other Austrian winter resorts have this type of funicular: Seefeld; St. Anton; Axamer Lizum; Ellmau; and Kaprun.

HARTKAISERBAHN

The winter resort town of Ellmau, is located on highway E17, about 10 miles east of the Salzburg-Innsbruck highway, in the heart of one of Austria's largest ski areas.

From the car park east of town, a large modern funicular, the Hartkaiserbahn, climbs 2427 feet to the summit of the Hartkaiser. Most of the line's 7708 feet of track is carried on a series of steel trusses to protect it against severe winter weather conditions.

Although intended primarily for skiers, the funicular also operates during the rest of the year for hikers and tourists. From the upper station and restaurant at 5085 feet, there are many wonderful views and, when the winter snows melt, the countryside lends itself to some great hiking.

The funicular operates hourly, 0800 till 1700, from June 15 until October 1 and from December 20 until March 30.

BERG BAHNEN ST. JOHANN

A short distance east of Ellmau at the intersection of highways E17 and 342 is the town of St. Johann in Tirol. Beautifully situated in a wide valley, St. Johann is both a winter and summer resort.

From a station at the base of the Kitzbuheler, the Berg Bahnen St. Johann, an 8016 foot long, two-stage funicular railway begins its climb to Angeralm (3933 feet). The first and longest of the two sections lifts you 823 feet to the middle station at Hochfeld (elev. 3073 feet). After changing to one of the cars

of the upper stage funicular, you ascend another
862 feet to the Bergstation at Angeralm. The
4270 foot long lower stage, has a maximum
gradient of 24% and is traveled in approximately
5 minutes. The upper section, although shorter
by 524 feet, is slightly steeper, having a
maximum gradient of 29%. As cable railways go,
this one is strictly minor league when it comes
to steepness. What it lacks in this area,
however, is more than made up for in beautiful
scenery. Whether winter skiing or summer
hiking, the area has much to offer and the
funicular takes you to where it all begins.

An aerial tramway, the Harschbichlbahn,
continues on up to Harschbichl at 5576 feet.
Fares range from 26 S for just one section of
the funicular to 100 S for both sections plus
the aerial tram.

The hours and months of operation are the
same as for the funicular at Ellmau.

ARLBERGER BERGBAHNEN

At the eastern end of the 6 1/2 mile long
Arlberg tunnel on route S16 is the picturesque
Tyrol village of St. Anton Am Arlberg. A well
known skiing and hiking holiday resort, its
funicular and aerial cableways operate year
round. During the winter, there are many miles
of ski slopes and cross country trails as well
as other facilities for winter sports. Summer
visitors have at their disposal over 50 miles of
trails, ranging from easy footpaths to the more
difficult alpine hiking trails and climbs.

From the center of St. Anton, near the OSS
gare, the Arlberger Bergbahen runs a funicular,
the Kandaharbahn, to the 6038 foot summit of
Gampen. Opened in 1973, the 4637 foot long route
takes you to the Bergstation Restaurant, where,
from the sun-terrace 1761 feet above the valley
floor, you are provided with marvelous views.

Whether covered with snow or blanketed with
lush green grass and wild flowers, the
countryside around St. Anton is always a
beautiful sight.

HUNGERBERGBAHN

From a station located at the northernmost
part of Innsbruck, the Hungerburgbahn climbs
941 feet to the village of Hungerburg (elev.
2847 feet). Spread out on an attractive plateau,
Hungerburg has a commanding view of the Inn

River, Innsbruck (Austria's winter capitol) and a sweeping panorama of alpine peaks.

Across from the upper station of the funicular is the lower station of the Nordkettenbahn, the cableway to Hafelekar, nearly 6000 feet higher. Whether you stay awhile at Hungerburg or go on to Hafelekar, you will find that there are dozens of scenic trails that extend for miles in many directions.

The base station of the funicular is at the river's edge, and, upon leaving the station, you immediately cross the river via a 518 foot long steel viaduct. With a maximum gradient of 55% and an average of nearly 50%, the cars travel the half-mile plus route in only 10 minutes. The ride is very enjoyable and offers wonderful sights all the way.

Many people choose to ride up on the funicular and then walk back down. The trail from Hungerburg to Innsbruck passes behind the Alpenzoo, the highest zoo in Europe and one that shouldn't be missed. The wooded path, surrounded by beautiful lush greenery, is moderately steep but not difficult to descend.

The Hungerbergbahn celebrated its 80th birthday in 1986, having started service in September of 1906.

The cars depart every 30 minutes or less, from about 0600 until 2230, year round. The fares are 24 S one-way and 36 S for a round trip.

OLYMPIABAHN

There is another funicular in the Innsbruck area at Axamer Lizum, the site of the skiing competition in two Olympics--1964 and 1976.

From the center of Innsbruck, you go south-west to the village of Axams, then southeast to the large car park at the end of the road. The station for the Olympiabahn, a very large and modern funicular, is right at the car park. Tall steel trusses carry the tracks for most of the 1-1/4 miles to the 7675 foot summit of Hoadle, a vertical distance of 2500 feet.

The panoramic view from the berg-station/restaurant is breathtaking. The bizarre peaks of the Kalkkogel mountain range fill your view to the south, and to the north, there is the city of Innsbruck on the Inn River.

The Lizum ski area is a natural bowl surrounded by a dozen or so peaks in the 8000 foot range. Their boast that during the winter, "snow is 100% guaranteed," is seldom wrong.

One way and round trip fares are 80 S and 120 S. Service is hourly from 0915 until 1425.

ACHENSEE ZAHNRADBAHN

If you're eastbound from Innsbruck on highways A12 or 171, a turn to the north about 6 miles past Schwaz will take you to the town of Jenbach. This is the rail-head for the Achensee Zahnradbahn, Europe's oldest rack railway operated exclusively by steam locomotives. Established in 1899, the meter gauge railway runs from Jenbach to Seespitz on the Achensee, Tirol's largest lake.

Pulling two or more coaches, the 5.4 mile long trip takes about 40 minutes, including the three intermediate stops at Burgeck, Eben and Maurach. Speed on the 2 mile section of Riggenbach rack is limited to 6 mph, while on the rest of the route it is 12 mph.

With a maximum gradient of 16% and a much lower average gradient, the route is not what you would call steep; however, you are lifted nearly 1400 feet during the trip. The ride is very enjoyable and one that is made by upwards of 75,000 persons each year.

The locomotives weigh in at 19 metric tons when full of water and ready to go. Both the engines and coaches have at least two braking systems independent of one another that can stop the train quickly and safely in case of emergency.

Trains operate daily from mid May through Sept. 30 and special group excursions can be arranged.

SEILBAHN SEEFELD-TIROL

Fiveteen miles northwest of Innsbruck, on the road toward Garmisch Partenkirchen, you will come to the resort town of Seefeld. The area affords fine skiing in the winter and excellent hiking during the summer months. There is also a wide variety of other activities for both seasons.

From the western edge of the city the Seilbahn Seefeld-Tirol AG ascends to Rosshutte (elev. 5773 feet). From the outdoor panoramic restaurant at the funicular's upper station, you are treated to magnificient views of the Inn Valley and the Zugspitze across the German border.

The two 120-passenger cars travel most of

the distance high above the ground on rails supported by steel trusses. The 8200 foot long route provides a lift of 1706 feet during the five minute ride.

Two aerial tram-ways depart from Rosshutte, one to Seefelder-Joch (elev. 6773 feet); the other to Harmilekopf, at 6691 feet. Operation is from mid-December to beginning of April and from the mid-May, to mid-October.

GOLMERBAHN

Seilbahn Seefeld-Tirol. (Tourist office Seefeld i. T.).

The Montafon Valley occupies the southwestern tip of Austria and lies between the world famous ski areas of Davos and Arlberg. Although relatively unknown to foreign skiers, it is very popular with Austrians as a family winter sports resort.

Departing from a station in the village of Latschau, a two stage funicular, Golmerbahn 1 and 2, climbs to Golm nearly 3000 feet above the valley floor. The station is easily reached by bus from Tschaggunn, the largest village in the valley.

The route of Golmerbahn 1 is the longest, at 4303 feet, and also the steepest, with an average gradient of 52%. The dividing point between the two sections is Matschwitz, where it is necessary to change cars if you wish to continue on. Golmerbahn 2 is 288 feet shorter than the lower section, but it still lifts you 1213 feet over a route that claims only a 38% gradient.

The 18 minute ride carries you through a pleasing mix of open meadows and lightly wooded countryside, as you glide along on the partly elevated route. There are restaurants at both the Matschwitz and Golm stations.

The 75-passenger cars run frequently from the end of May to the middle of October and then again from mid-December, to mid-April. The round trip fare in 1986 was 95 S.

VERMUNTBAHN

From the village of Partenen, at the extreme southern end of the Montafon Valley, another funicular climbs nearly 3000 feet to Trominier at 5674 feet.

The 4723 foot long route of the Vermuntbahn is steep (64%) and wooded much of the way. As you pass through the cleared areas, however, the open car provides unobstructed and spectacular views of the valley below. The 20 minute ascent terminates at Trominier, where you will find a well supplied snack bar.

From the upper station, a bus, "the Tunnel Taxi", will take you via a scenic road, that includes several tunnels, naturally, to the Berghotel Bielerhohe at silvrettasee, elev. 7560 feet. The modern hotel occupies a beautiful setting overlooking the large lake. Boat trips are available during the summer only as the lake freezes over in the winter. The hotel can also be reached by auto from Partenen.

Silvrettasee is the Montafon's jumping off point for ski touring and heli-skiing into Switzerland. During the summer, thousands of hikers come to enjoy the miles of fine trails through the beautiful mountain scenery.

The round trip fare for just the Vermuntbahn is 65 S, but, if you wish include a round trip to the hotel via the "Tunnel Taxi", add another 115 S.

GLETSCHERBAHN

The Grossglockner Alpine Highway, reported to be the most scenic N/S route across the Alps, is also a masterpiece of road building technology.

From the town of Bruck in the Salzak Valley, the highway leads south, crosses the 8300 foot Hochtor, and continues on to the picturesque Alpine village of Heiligenblut, 30 miles distant.

At the Edelwleisshuette, located just one mile off the highway at about the 17 mile point, there is a car park with an outlook tower. On a clear day, it is possible from that one spot to see as many as 19 glaciers and 37 mountain peaks, each one exceeding 10,000 feet in height.

Farther on at mile 25, a turn to the left at the Guttal bridge will put you on the Gletscherstrasse or Glacier Road. After 4 very scenic miles you will arrive at the Franz-Joseph-Hohe (elev.7728 feet), where you will have an unobstructed view of the famous Pasterze Glacier and the imposing 12,457 Grossglockner.

From the car park, a funicular descends 473 feet down the steep cliff to the glacier below. When the cable railway was constructed in 1962/63, the lower station was at the edge of the ice. The glacier has since receded, however, so now it is necessary to walk a short distance to the ice.

The Grossglockner-Gletscherbahn (Glacier

The Gletscherbahn (Glacier Railway) with a gradient of 95.5%, is Europe's steepest conventional funicular. (Glossglockner Gletscher

Railway) is the steepest conventional funicular in Europe, having a maximunm gradient of 95.5%. With four sets of brakes, each independent of the others, the system is quite safe in spite of the steepness.

The little glass enclosed cars carry 32 passengers in 3 compartments and make the 695 foot long trip in 2 minutes. The fare is 50 S round trip or 35 S one-way. It isn't uncommon for people to take the funicular just one direction and hike the other.

KAPRUN VALLEY

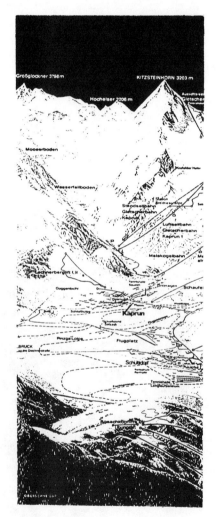

Driving west from Bruck you will come to Zell am See and the mouth of the Kaprun valley. The valley is the site of one of Austria's largest hyrdro-electric projects, which taps the runoff from the Pasterze Glacier.

The Moll River, the headwater of which is the pasterze Glacier, flows into the Margaritze reservoir (elev. 6622 feet) at the base of the Grossglockner. From there, water is sent through a seven mile long tunnel to the Mooserboden reservoir (elev. 6560 feet) behind the Mooser and Drossen dams. After being used to create electrical power, the water flows down into the Wasserfallboden reservoir, created by the Limberg dam. Water from here is also used to generate electricity, but, when there is a surplus of energy, water is ocassionally pumped back up to the mooserboden reservoir to be used over again during high usage periods.

Up stream from Kaprun there are no fewer than seven cable railways, including the Larchwand, the world's largest. The Larchwand and some of the others are more accurately called inclined cable lifts and consist only of a platform held horizontal by a wedge shaped rail car. In other words, a wedge-tram type funicular minus the tram car. All but one of the cable railways in the Kaprun Valley were built to carry supplies and men for the construction of the dams.

MISKOGEL-SCHRAGAUFZUG

On the west side of the river, as you start up the valley, you will come upon the Krafthaus Kaprun and the lower station of the Maiskogel-Schragaufzug. Equipped with seats and a roof, but no sides, this incline lift at least resembles a funicular to some degree. As It

(Above) Pushing a single passenger car, a steam locomotive of the Schrafberg Railway approaches the station at the Schrafbergspitze at 3897 feet elevation. (O.B.B.).

(Below) With a track gauge of 27 feet and a capacity of 60 metric tons, the Larchwandaufzug is reported to be the world's largest incline railway. Its steep route (70%) lifts you 1413 feet above the floor of the Kaprun Valley. (Werksgruppe Glockner-Kaprun tauernkraftwerke AG).

climbs the steep mountainside, its 5 foot 3 inch gauge tracks run parallel to the pipes carrying water from wasserfallboden.

With a maximum gradient of 82%, the 4736 foot long route to the Maiskogelhutte lifts you 2766 feet. The Hutte can also be reached via an aerial tram that departs from the valley a short distance from the station of the schragaufzug.

GLETSCHERBAHN KAPRUN 2

Gletcherbahn Kaprun 2 at its lower station. The first 1950 feet of the route span the the Kaprun river via the tall steel bridge pictured above. (Gletscherbahnen Kaprun).

A drive of about three miles up the valley will put you at the station of Gletscherbahn 2, or G-BK 2, as it is known. One of the longest funicular railways anywhere and one of the largest in terms of passenger capacity, it is also the only cable line of the lot that was built strictly for winter sports.

As the huge car departs the lower station, it immediately starts its ascent up a 1950 foot steel bridge and disappears into a tunnel. Two miles and nine minutes later, it reappears at the Alpencenter (elev. 8036 feet), having climbed nearly one mile in approximately 10 minutes.

Except for the very beginning, the trip could hardly be called scenic; however, the view from the Alpencenter more than makes up for that shortcoming. With the peaks of the 10,501 foot high Kitzsteinhorn, and the 12,457 foot Grossglockner as backdrops, the view is nothing short of spectacular.

The base station of the funicular is also the starting point for the G-BK1, an aerial cableway that goes to the Alpencenter via Salzburger Hutte. From the Center, another cableway continues on to the 9935 foot level of the Kitzsteinhorn where there is a restaurant and something called a "panorama-tunnel."

SCHRAGAUFZUG LIMBERSTOLLEN

From Kesselfall Alpenhaus, a 9184 foot long inclined tunnel, the Limbergstollen leads to the base of the Limberg dam. Inside the tunnel, which was built as a winter route to the dam site, the Schragaufzug Limbergstollen travels 3027 feet up the incline at a gradient of 87%, providing a lift of 1912 feet to the Krafthaus Limberg in just over seven minutes.

SCHRAGAUFZUG LIMBERG WEST

A short walk from there, will take you to the base station of the Schragaufzug Limberg West. With a maximum gradient of 119%, it is probably the steepest inclined railway you will ever ride. Carrying 12 passengers, or a total maximum weight of 2 metric tons, it climbs the 430 feet to the crest of the dam in 15 minutes. The over-all length of the climb is 610 feet.

SCHRAGAUFZUG LIMBERG EAST

From the east rim of the dam, the Schragaufzug Limberg East, with a max. gradient of 90%, carries 8 passengers at a time to the upper valves chamber: a change in elevation of 846 feet over the 1312 foot route. With a full load of passengers, the trip takes 3 minutes and 42 seconds.

SCHRAGAUFZUG MOLLPUMPWERK

The last of the inclined cable lifts directly connected with the dams is the Schragaufzug Mollpumpwerk, which has a load limit of 20 metric tons, or up to 48 passengers. Starting from the Moll pumping station at the Mooserboden reservoir, it ascends 318 feet to the rim of the Drossen dam. The climb up the 525 foot long incline takes between 7 and 9 minutes, depending on the load.

Making the complete circut of the dams is not only an interesting experience but also a very scenic trip--aside from the tunnel lifts, of course.

LARCHWANDAUFZUG

A little beyond the Kesselfall Alpenhaus on the opposite side of the valley, the Larchwandaufzug, the world's largest incline railway, starts it's ascent. It's tracks, which are just short of being 27 feet apart, support a platform car with a capacity of 60 metric tons of equipment or room for 140 standing passengers.

Starting from the Larchwand route in the valley, the lift climbs steeply (70%) to the middle station at Limbergstrasse, located about

1/2 mile from the base of the Limberg dam and on the same level. Continuing on to the upper station, you arrive at the start of Mooserbodenstrasse 1413 feet above the valley. This very scenic road will take you to the crest of the Limberg dam and then along the shore of the wasserfallboden reservoir before climbing up to the rim of the Mooser dam. There is a bus service from the upper station that covers the route, but one should inquire in advance about the availability of the service. The length of the route of the Larchwandaufzug is 2663 feet and the time required to cover the distance varies from 9 minutes for a full load of passengers, to 36 minutes for a 60 ton load of equipment.

SALZBERGBAHN

To truly appreciate the magnificient setting of Hallstatt Am See, take the funicular to the summit of the Salzberg. From the restaurant adjoining the upper station 1050 feet above the town, you are treated to breathtaking views of the surrounding mountains and shimmering blue lake that lies below.

In 1981, the Salzbergbahn replaced an aerial gondola that had operated there for 25 years, and now offers a thrilling ride as it makes its steep ascent in only 3 minutes. The funicular operates only from April through October and the round trip fare is 50 S.

SCHLOSSALM STANSEILBAHN

The small "wedge-tram" style car of the Salzberg-bahn nearing the top end of the passing loop. (Salzbergbahn/Hallstatt).

The winter resort town of Bad Hofgastein lies nearly due east of Grossglockner on the other side of the Goldberg Grouppe, a mountain range boasting three or four peaks in the 9,000 to 10,000 foot range. It can be reached from Zell am Zee, by heading east on highway 311 to Lend, then south on highway 167.

In 1984 the town celebrated the 20th anniversary of their new funicular, the Schlossalm Standseilbahn. Traveling mostly above ground on a series of raised steel trusses, the large modern cars of the 4231 foot long cable railway lift you 1508 feet to Kitzstein. Aerial cable cars continue on up the mountain to Kleine Scharte, at 6744 feet.

The present funicular replaced a previous one built in 1946 which, although still in good condition, did not have enough carrying capacity

An engine and car of the Schneebergbahn standing at the 5888-foot summit station of Hochschneeberg, Austria's highest railway station. (O.B.B.).

The two original cars of the Grazer Schloss-bergbahn, which started service in 1894. (H. Wober/Wien).

for the busy area. Operation is from November 29 to April 20, with cars departing Bad Hofgastein and Kitzstein about every 15 minutes from 0800 until 1600. Round trip fare is 60S.

FESTUNGSBAHN

If you've never ridden on the Festungsbahn, you've probably never been to Salzburg. Each year more than a million people make the trip to and from Hohensalzburg Fortress via the little cable railway. Being in Salzburg and not visiting that historic landmark, would be like a trip to Pisa without seeing the famous leaning tower.

From its inception in 1892 until it was electrified in 1959, the Festungsbahn was a hydraulically operated funicular, equipped with a Riggenback rack and pinion system. Now, with over 95 years of service, it is Austria's oldest existing funicular and the only one to have ever reached 90 years of age.

It departs from a station at # 4 Festungstrasse and unless required to stop at Mounchburg, reaches the fortress in 90 seconds. The route is rather steep, having an average gradient of 55% and reaching 61% at one point. This accounts for the 325 foot lift accomplished over the 623 foot long course. The single-car funicular railway is capable of carrying up to 860 passengers during its 12 round trips each hour.

The fortress is open to the public for a fee, and there is a nice panoramic restaurant where you can relax and enjoy some fine scenery. Many people walk back down the hill, but it isn't recommended for everyone.

SCHRAFBERG RAILWAY

Austria's second rack railway begins its ascent from the town of St. Wolfgang, situated approximately 30 miles south east of Salzburg. Known as the Schafberg Railway, the 3.5 mile long, narrow gauge (1000mm) line climbs from St. Wolfgang to Schafbergspitze, a change in elevation of 3897 feet. Pushing a single passenger car, the small kneeling-type steam locomotive ascends the 25% gradient in approximately one hour. The route, which is equipped with an Abt rack, also accomodates the company's modern diesel rail cars that make the trip in only 39 minutes.

Construction on the railway started in 1892 and was accomplished by 350 Italian workmen in the amazing time of slightly over one year. Six thousand mule loads of equiupment, food and other supplies had to be hauled up the mountain to the construction site. The route includes a 78 foot long viaduct, several rock bridges, numerous cuts through solid rock and two tunnels (298 feet and 85 feet in length).

A small refuge hut for skiers and hikers was built on the summit of the Schafberg sometime before 1839. In 1906, the hut was replaced by a hotel and in 1948, the hotel was renovated and enlarged to the state it is in today. In addition to accomodations for 70 overnight guests, it has two dining rooms, a bar and an outdoor panoramic restaurant that offers spectacular views of St. Wolfgang See and the surrounding mountain peaks.

There are two passing points on the route, the first at Dorneralpe (1.6 miles, elev. 3411 feet), and the other at Schafbergalpe (2.5 miles, elev. 4471 feet). Water for the locomotives is available at both locations. Schafbergalpe, with trails heading off in several directions, is also a favorite starting point for many hikers.

The Schrafberg Railway now has five steam locomotives that have been in continuous use since they were acquired in 1893-1894. Owned by the OBB, the Schafberg's locomotives are numbered from 999.102 to 999.106. Their original engine, which was 999.101, is now with the Schneebergbahn. The company's engines are also named: .102 is "Enzian;" .103 "Erika;" .104 "Bergprimel;" .105 "Almrausch;" and .106 "Berganemone." Other rolling stock includes two diesel-hydraulic rail cars from 1964 and several passenger coaches built about the same time as the steam engines. The railcars can carry 74 passengers each, as opposed to the steam trains which have a maximum capacity of 60 persons.

Service is daily from early May to mid-October, with trains leaving Wolfgang at about forty five minute intervals, starting at approximately 0800 and continuing until 1800. During the peak season, the first train departs a little earlier and additional trips are made each day.

One-way and round trip fares for adults are: 92/168 S; for children, the fare is 76 S each way.

SCHNEEBERGBAHN

Less than an hour's driving time from Vienna, at Puchberg am Schneeberg, is the last of Austria's three popular rack railways. Known alternately as the "Hochschneebergbahn", "Schneebergbahn," or "Puchberg Zahnradbahn," it has been climbing the Schneeberg since 1897. The little railway is the center of attraction, even in this renown health and winter sports resort, and is partially responsible for the areas reputation as the "Chamonix of Austria."

Departing from the center of Puchberg am Scheeberg and employing a Strub rack, the train climbs the eastern slope of the mountain as far as Baumgartner and then follows the ridge to the summit station, which at 5888 feet, is the highest in Austria. The average gradient on the 5.8 mile long route is about 12%, with a maximum of 20%. There are two tunnels and five scheduled stops along the route, including a stop at Baumgartner to take on water. The area is often referred to as a hiker's paradise and well marked trails radiate from most stops.

Before actual construction started, several other routes to the summit were suggested, but the present one was chosen in 1895 and construction was started on the line soon afterwards. The line was completed to Baumgartner on June 6, 1897 and to Hochschneeberg on October 25 of the same year. The railway became part of the OBB in 1937.

Rolling stock consists of six steam locomotives of the kneeling type, and several vintage passenger coaches.

The trains run daily, departing Puchberg at 0710 on Fridays, Saturdays and Sundays, and at 0710 on the other days of the week. During the month of May, the train leaves Puchberg at 1545 on Fridays, Saturdays and Sundays and at 1140 the rest of the week. Adult fares are: 80 S one-way and 140 S round trip. Children 6-15 go for half price and seniors pay 126 S for a round trip.

GRAZER SCHLOSSBERGBAHN

Founded in the year 1115 along the banks of the River Mur, Graz is now Austria's second largest city. Rising some 340 feet above the city is the Schlossberg, a dominent feature of Graz and one that is visable from nearly every part of the city. Only the clock tower, built in 1561, and the bell tower, from 1588, remain to remind one of the great fortress that once occupied that strategic site.

From the Franz-Josef Kai at the end of Sack Strass, a funicular railway begins its ascent to the summit of the Schlossberg. The steep, 668-foot long route of the Grazer Schlossbergbahn takes the form of a continuous curve as it climbs the woooded hillside. The cars, which carry a maximum of 46 passengers including 16 standing, lift you 340 feet during the scenic 3 minute ride.

When the railway was first completed in 1894, it followed a slightly different route than it does at present. Also, steam was generated in a boiler at the lower station and piped to the top of the hill, where it was used to run the steam engine that lifted the cars. A Riggenback rack and pinion system, with a special clamping device, was used to aid in braking and to insure that the cars didn't lift off the tracks. During its 66 years of service, there was not a single serious accident.

In 1900, the line was electrified and, in 1960, the old Schlossbergbahn was retired to make room for the new modernized version.

The funicular operates year-round on a daily basis, with frequent departures all day. The views from either of the towers at the summit are exceptional.

The modern cars of the present-day Schlossberg-bahn on the passing loop. (H. Wober//Wien).

G E R M A N
FUNICULAR AND RACK RAILWAYS

1 BERGBAHN HEIDELBERG
2 NEROBERGBAHN WIESBADEN
3 WENDELSTEIN ZAHNRADBAHN
4 BAYERISCHE ZUGSPITZBAHN

CHAPTER THREE

GERMAN
FUNICULAR AND RACK RAILWAYS

Unlike its neighbors Switzerland, Austria, and France, Germany has only two rack and pinion railways and two funiculars. It does, however, have one of only two water balance funiculars remaining in Europe. Also, as you will see in a later chapter, Germany has an abundance of steam railways.

BERGBAHN HEIDELBERG

The city of Heidelberg is probably best known as the home of Heidelberg University, one of the oldest and most prestigious in the world. The main tourist attraction in this colorful city on the Nekar river, however, is the partially restored castle on the hill overlooking the city.

There are a number of ways to get to the castle, but the most popular and enjoyable route is via the Funicular Bergbahn Heidelberg. The trip which begins at the Kornmarkt, takes only two minutes and a round trip costs but 3.50 DM. Actually the fare includes an additional two minute ride on up to Molkenkur and return.

The first, or lower, section of the two-stage Bergbahn Heidelberg was inaugerated on March 30, 1890 and, except for a few interruptions, has been in service ever since. It was originally constructed as a water balance funicular with a Riggenbach rack and it remained that way until it was electrified in 1905. Although the railway is approaching its hundredth birthday, it has been modernized a great deal and today is like new.

The 1604 foot long route begins at the Kornmarkt station, makes a stop at the castle and then goes on up to Molkenkur (elev. 939 feet), a change in elevation of 567 feet.

From Molkenkur, but from a separate station, the second stage of the funicular departs for Konigsthul (elev. 1803 feet). This section, which is by far the longest at 3346 feet, provides a lift of 853 feet in only 9 minutes. The handsome wooden cars, that are presently in use on this section, are the very same ones that were in use on the first day of service, June 1, 1907.

The trip from the Kornmarkt to Molkenkur provides many fine views, but from the castle the view of the city is unsurpassed. From Molkenkur to Konigsthul, the route is pretty well closed in by the woods and, although very scenic, provides no view until you arrive at the upper station. Near the upper station there is a tall TV tower that can be ascended for some spectacular views of the Nekar Valley, Rhein Plain and the Odenwald.

Both funiculars run about every 40 minutes from 0900 until 1900, except in winter when the hours of service are a little shorter. The round trip fares are: Kornmarkt-Molkenkur, 3.50 DM; Molkenkur-Konigsthul, 3.50 DM; Kornmarkt-Konigsthul, 5.50 DM. The travel time for a round trip on both sections of the funicular, is approximately 35 minutes.

The total length of the cable railway is 4950 feet.

NEROBERGBAHN WIESBADEN

The hydraulically operated Nerobergbahn Wiesbaden is one of only two such cable railways in all of western Europe. Locally it is referred to as a rack railway, but it is definitely a funicular. It does employ a Riggenbach rack and pinion system, but, as is the case with many other funiculars, The rack it is used only for braking purposes.

Operated by the ESWE, Wiesbaden's bus and utility company, the 1438 foot long railway connects the Nerotal Valley with the summit of the Neroberg, which overlooks the city. Nearing its hundredth birthday, the little meter gauge funicular is a piece of living history for the city and has operated without a single accident since the days of Emperor Wilhelm The fact that it has four independently operated braking systems and a moderate 25% gradient could account for that remarkable record.

A car of the Bergbahn Heidelberg
on the lower section of the two-
stage funicular. (Tourist Office,
Heidelberg).

One of the old-time cars of the
Nerobergbahn, Germany's one and only
"water "balance" funicular.
ESWE Stadtwerk Wiesbaden. (A. Fay).

The electric-powered
Wendelstein Zahnrad-
bahn approaching the
summit of the 5680-
foot Wendelstein.
The gradient at this
point is nearly 25%.
(M. Weiss).

The attractive open ended, yellow and blue cars lift you 263 feet, amid some lovely scenery, during the course of the short (3-1/4 minutes) ride.

On the summit there are several attractions, including a large outdoor swimming pool, a cafe and restaurant and even a Greek temple. On a clear day it is possible to see all the way to Mainz.

Each car has a water capacity of 7000 liters and the only energy required to raise and lower the cars is a small pump to return the water to the top station. The popular cable railway has interlaced tracks above and below the passing loop

Service is every 15 minutes, from approximately 1000 to 1900 during the period from Easter until the end of october. The fare is 1 DM each way.

WENDELSTEIN ZAHNRADBAHN

The 4-1/2 mile long, meter gauge railway, Wendelstein Zahnradbahn, runs from the village of Brannenburg in S/E Germany to the summit of the 5680-foot Wendelstein. Powered by either a 1912 or 1925 vintage electric engine, the 50-passenger yellow and white cars of the Wendelstein Zahnradbahn make the 4015 foot ascent in 55 minutes.

The slope is gentle as you leave the Brannenburg station and you are on adhesion until just before making the first sharp turn to the right. The first rack section (Strub), which is 1.6 miles long, takes you beyond the first stop at Gembachau. The second, and longer, of the two rack sections starts at Aipl, which is the middle station and the passing point for ascending and descending trains. Shortly after a stop at Mitteralm, you will enter the first of six tunnels, the last of which will put you at the summit station.

With an average gradient of over 20%, and reaching 25% in a few places, the course of this combination adhesion/rack line is quite steep. Less than one mile of the route is adhesion, with most of that being in the area of the passing loop at Aipl. In addition to the six tunnels near the summit, there are eight snow galleries to protect the train as it skirts the sheer cliffs. There are also twelve bridges along the route.

Lush forests and meadows, punctuated by deep valleys and beautiful mountain scenery, make this a spectacular and memorable trip.

From the upper station, an underground passageway leads to the hotel and station of the aerial tram from Bayrischzell. Wendelstein is one of the most popular winter ski sites in the country and the restaurant at the summit provides some of the best viewing in Germany.

Before and after the skiing season, the more than twenty well-marked trails in the larger Wendelstein area are used by thousands of serious and recreational hikers.

The trains runs hourly from 0900 until about 1500 in the winter, and to 1700 in the summer. Adult fares are 18 DM for one-way and 29 DM for the round trip. Children 8-12 go for half price when accompanied by adults. There are also several combinations of fares for going one way by train and the other by aerial tram, etc. In addition, there are daily, weekly and season tickets, during the winter season.

Brannenberg can be reached by taking highway 171, or the autobahn (A12), north from the Salzburg-Innsbruck highway, between the towns of Ellmau and Jenbach.

BAYERISCHE ZUGSPITZBAHN

The Bayerische Zugspitzbahn, Germany's other rack railway, is also a meter gauge, combination rack/adhesion line. Inaugurated on December 12, 1929, the 11.1 mile long Riggenbach-equipped railway climbs 1950 feet up the famous Zugspitz, reaching gradients of up to 25%.

Departing from Garmisch-Partenkirchen on adhesion, it makes stops at Riessersee, Hammersbach, and Grainau, a distance of 4.5 miles, in 19 minutes. At Grainau it goes onto the 6.5 mile long rack section to start the ascent. The first stop on the rack section is at Eibsee, which is the starting point of the Eibsee aerial tram that goes all the way to the 10,000 foot summit of the Zugspitz. At Riffelriss, the last intermediate stop, the train goes into a 2.7 mile long tunnel that ends at Schneefernerhaus, elev. 8700 feet.

Very modern and powerful electric locomotives, pulling as many as seven cars, make the trip from Garmisch in one hour and 15 minutes. Except for the long tunnel section, the trip is one of great beauty and the view from Germany's highest restaurant is magnificient.

The trains run hourly from 0800 and continue until 1500 or later, depending on the time of year. It is also possible to start the trip from most any of the intermediate stops

along the way. Departure for descending trains
are also hourly from 1000 until 1600 or later,
also depending on the time of year.

The adult fare for a round trip from
Garmisch is 42 DM. A combination round trip,
using the Zugspitzbahn one way and the aerial
tram the other, is 40 DM. Children's tickets
cost 26 DM and 24 DM respectively. Fares from
other starting points and several other
combination tickets are also available.

Garmisch-Partenkirchen is situated close to
the Austrian border and can be reached via
highway 2 from Innsbruck.

Departing from Garmisch-Partenkirchen, the Bayerische
Zugspitzbahn, Germany's premier rack and pinion railway,
begins its climb to the 8700-foot level of the famous
Zugspitz. (BZB archive photo by Huber)

CHAPTER FOUR

INTRODUCTION
TO STEAM RAILWAYS

Europeans, as you may already have heard, take great pride in their railways which are well known for their on-time service, comfort and reliability. The same pride that is evident in their operation of the larger railways is also present on the steam trains, where providing the passengers with a safe and pleasant trip is their highest priority. The men who drive the steam trains are generally volunteer members of a railway organization and, more often than not, are active or retired railway engineers.

Depending on which country you're in, you will find that the railways are referred to as "Museumbahns," "Chemin de Fer Touristique," or just plain, "Tourist Trains."

With but a few exceptions, each of the museum and tourist railways are owned and operated by one of the many railway associations. The exceptions are a very small number that are privately owned, a few government owned, and some that are run by larger railways over their regular routes.

Soon after World War II ended, a massive rebuilding of the industrial nations began. The railways, which had been heavily damaged and had had their equipment severely depleted, were in the forefront of the rebuilding program. As modern electric and diesel engines and new passenger cars became available, hundreds of steam locomotives and vintage coaches all over Europe were sent to the scrap heap or left on out-of-the-way sidings to rust away.

As the steam locomotives started to become conspicuous by their absence, railway enthusiasts, especially those with a love for steam engines, started to band together to save as many as possible. In Austria, Germany, Switzerland, France and, in fact, in most of the European Countries, railway associations for the preservation and display of railway memorabilia sprang up like wildfire.

At first, the emphasis was mainly on collecting, preserving and restoring steam locomotives, but it soon expanded to include anything and everything related to railways of the past.

The end of the war also saw the beginning of an enormous upsurge in the use of trucks and cars for the intercity transportation of goods and passengers. Over the next thirty years, short line railways, some of which had been in service for more than a hundred years but not able to meet the new competition, were being abandoned in ever increasing numbers. It was not only bad news for the railways but also for the passengers who depended on their service.

Sometimes bad news for one is good news for another, and so it was with the closing of some of the short lines. For any railway association with rolling stock and looking for a place to start a tourist railway, the closing of a line, although sad, was, nevertheless, a golden oportunity. It took an enormous amount of money, work and determination to get a railway, even a tourist railway, out of the museum and onto the tracks, but many of the organizations accomplished just that.

From year to year, there is a slight variation in the number of tourist railways operating in Europe, but the number probably seldom falls below one hundred. This figure does not include the numerous museum tramways or tourist trains powered by other than steam.

All of the railways and routes covered in this book were in service during the 1987 season and there is good reason to believe they will continue to operate in the future.

Information for this book was obtained through personal visits to the railways and extensive correspondence. Although great effort was made to include every steam railway in Austria and Germany, the language difference, and other causes prevented that from becoming a reality.

Wherever possible, the address is given where one can write for current time, date and fare information. Be aware, however, that the information you receive will not necessarily be in English. Your chances for an English translation are sometimes greatly improved, if your letter is accompanied by one or two International Postage Coupons.

The standard gauge
Montafonerbahn, with
steam locomotive
178.84, making its
way between Bludenz
and Schruns. (MBS).

Zillertalbahn engine
#5 "Gerlos" pulling
several vintage cars
as it steams through
the beautiful
Zillertal Valley
(Zillertaler Verkehrs-
betriebe AG).

35

A U S T R I A N STEAM RAILWAYS

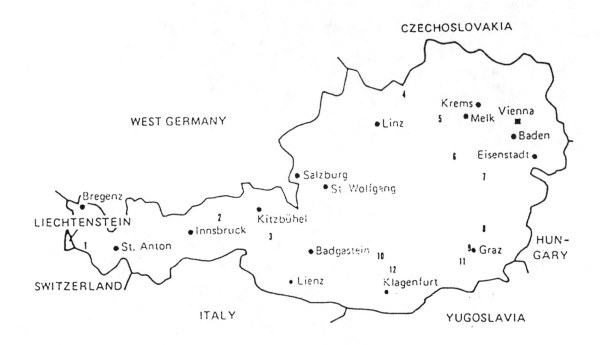

1 MONTAFONERBAHN
2 ZILLERTALBAHN
3 PINZGAUER BAHN
4 WALDVIERTELBAHNEN
5 YBBSTALBAHN
6 MARIANZELLERBAHN

7 MUSEUMISENBAHN PAYERBACH-
   REICHENAU-HIRSCHWANG
8 FEISTRITZTALBAHN
9 GRAZ-KOFLACHER EISENBAHN
10 MURTALBAHN
11 STAINZERBAHN
12 GURKTALBAHN

CHAPTER FIVE

AUSTRIAN STEAM RAILWAYS

In addition to Austria's national railway, which goes by the name Osterreichische Bundesbahnen (OBB), Austria has a large number of other railways. They include: several small railways that are owned by the OBB, but which operate under different names; nearly all of the funiculars and rack railways; numerous small secondary lines; plus, the subject of this chapter, steam railways--most of which are owned by associations of rail enthusists.

MONTAFONERBAHN

Not far from both the Swiss and Liechtenstein borders, a standard gauge railway, the Montafonerbahn, runs steam trains over a 7.8 mile route.

Starting from the OBB Bahnhof in Bludenz, located on the main autoroute leading west from Innsbruck, the route goes south to the winter resort town of Schruns. As you travel down the valley of the Ill river, crossing it a time or two, towering mountains and lovely evergreen forests fill your view. Although short in distance and duration, one would be hard pressed to find a more beautiful and relaxing train ride. The trip each way takes only twenty to thirty minutes, even though the train makes several stops. A photo stop is also quite often made at some point along the route.

The line came into existance in 1905 and was the first electric railway in the Austro-Hungarian empire. As with many of the railways, electric trains are used on the route throughout the year, with steam trains being added during

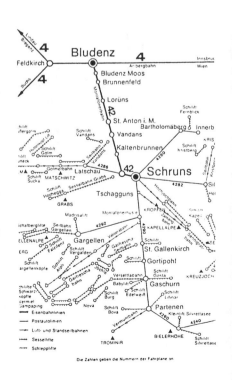

the Summer for tourists and rail fans.

The steam train runs every Thursday, from mid-June to mid-September, but the departure schedule is not available at this time. Round trip fares for adults and children are 40 S and 20 S. Special group trips and a "hobby train" are also available. The trip is made some thirty times a day by the electric trains but only once or twice a day by the steam train. The schedule is #42 in the Kursbuch.

The company's rolling stock includes the following: one steam locomotive, # 178.84, built in 1909 and used for all the steam excursions and the "hobby train"; nine or ten electric and about the same number of diesel engines; and a large number of passenger, freight and miscellaneous rail vehicles.

For additional information, write: Montafon-erbahn AG Betriebsleitung, Batlogstrasse 45, 6780 Schruns, Austria.

ZILLERTALBAHN

Jenbach, besides being the rail-head for the Achenseebahn, mentioned in chapter two, is also the starting point for the steam powered Zillertalbahn. An underpass, which takes you under the tracks of the OBB, connects the Zillertal and Achensee stations.

Jenbach hosts three railways, each with different gauge tracks: the OBB with its 1235mm gauge; the 1000mm gauge Achensee Zahnradbahn; and the 760mm gauge Zillertalbahn.

When inaugurated in December of 1900, the line, with only two locomotives and a handful of other cars, ran from Jenbach to Fugen. The following year it was extended, first to Kaltenbach, then to Erlach, and, finally, to Zell am Ziller. The final link to Mayrhofer was completed on July 31, 1902. One of the two original steam engines, locomotive #2, "Zillertal," built in 1902, is still in use. The other original engine, #1, "Raimund," has been in the rail museum in Innsbruck since 1970.

The 19 mile trip through the Zillertal region is very scenic, with most of the towns lying between 1600 and 5000 feet, and protected from strong winds by the higher mountains. With hiking being a popular pastime here, as in most parts of Austria, one can easily find foot paths leading in just about any direction. Some of the paths and trails take you through heavily forested areas and some, lead to as high as 10,000 feet.

All Aboard! The narrow gauge Pinzgauer Bahn prepares to depart on its 32 mile trip from Zell-am See to Krimml. (Pinzgauer Bahn).

Nearly 43 miles of grand scenery is in store for passengers of the narrow gauge Ybbstalbahn. Shown is engine # 598.02 (1896) crossing the Huhner-nestgraben trestle bridge. (Club 598).

Steam train of the standard gauge Mariazellerbahn. In operation from June to October, the museum railway connects Mariazell with the Erlaufsee. (Museumbahn Mariazell-Erlaufsee. Fotoverlag Cermak).

Although trains operate on the route all year round, steam locomotives are used only from the beginning of June to the end of September. The trip takes about one hour and fifteen minutes, including a minimum of nine stops en route. Trains depart from Jenbach at 1055 and 1540 and from Mayrhofen at 1235 and 1729. To add to the atmosphere of the train ride, the members of the train crew all wear the historic, turn-of-the-century uniforms.

Depending on the number of passengers, the steam trains usually consist of two or three vintage coaches, a bar car and a buffet wagon. The bar car, which is shaped like a giant beer barrel, is called the "Fassel Wagon" and can accomodate up to 20 persons.

In addition to the regularly scheduled trains, there is a "Hobby Train" for those who would like the thrill of taking over the controls of a live steam locomotive. This train is run over the relatively short distance between Zell am Ziller and Mayrhofen and return. The cost is rather high, but you do get an attractive certificate attesting to your achievement. With advanced notice, special trips can also be arranged for groups during other than the regular times. During the Christmas and New Year's holidays, steam trains are often included in the festivities.

One-way and round trip fares between Jenbach and Mayrhofen are 28 S and 48 S. The cost for driving the steam train from Zell am Zeller to Mayrhofen, is 300 S one-way, or 540 S round trip. The "Hobby Train" can also be reserved by a group for 2700 S an hour. Other fares on request.

The railway's rolling stock now includes: four steam locomotives, from 1900-1939; six diesel locomotives, all dating from the late 1969s and 1970s; three diesel railcars; 28 passenger coaches; three baggage cars; and 67 freight cars.

For additional information or reservations, write: Zillertaler Verkehrsbetriebe AG, A-6200 Jenbach/Tirol, Austria.

PINZGAUER BAHN

Zell am See is also the terminus of the Pinzgauer Bahn, a narrow gauge (760mm) railway operated by the OBB. The company operates with diesel engines throughout the year but also runs steam trains over the line during the summer months. The 32-mile long route between Zell am See and Krimml, follows the valley of the Salzach River through an area known as Oberpinzgau. Surrounded by magnificient alpine peaks including Austria's mightiest, the 12,454 foot high Grossglockner, the trip ranks as one of the most scenic in Austria.

In 1896, the "Pinzgauer Lokalbahn-gellschaft" was awarded the concession to build and operate a railway betweeen Zell am See and Krimml. In less than two years, the company accumulated rolling stock, built the line and started service. During World War 2 the railway was run by the Deutsche Reichsbahn (DR), but became part of the OBB in 1945 when the German occupation of Austria ended.

Steam train service is offered on Tuesdays and Thursdays in July and August and also on Saturdays during September. Because of the rather long duration of the trip approximately 2 hours 15 minutes, fares are based on portions of the trip and can be purchased for either one-way or round trip. One-way adult fares are: (1-15 Km), 50 S; (16-35 Km), 90 S; (36-54 Km), 130 S. Round trips are 80 S, 130 S and 190 S, respectively. Children 6-15 years of age pay half price. In addition, there are family fares, group fares and package fares for special excursions that include dinner and a side trip to the Krimmler Waterfalls. Incidentally, there are three waterfalls within walking distance of the station in Krimml.

The train departs from Zell am See at 0915 and arrives in Krimml at 1140. The return trip from Krimml begins at 1555, arriving back at Zell am See at 1812. With fourteen intermediate stops along the way, and the long layover in Krimml, passengers have a wide choice of stopping places and plenty of time for hiking or exploring the area of their choice.

The Zell am See and Kaprun areas are important winter sports resorts and offer every amenity for both winter and summer fun.

For additiional information, write: Pinzgauer Bahn, A-5724 Stuhlfelden, Austria.

WALDVIERTELBAHNEN

Austria's most northern steam railway is the 760mm gauge Waldviertelbahnen, which originates in the town of Gmund on the Czechoslovakian border. When opened for business in 1902, the line made a connection with the Franz Josefs-Bahn which, for many years, joined Vienna and Prague.

Starting from Gmund, the largest of several towns on the 25.8 mile long route, the train

climbs slowly to the town of Weitra, well-known
for its large Renaissance castle and other
notable structures. Upon departing Weitra, you
will cross a picturesque, seven arch stone
viaduct before reaching the idyllic village of
St. Martin bei Weitra. Soft, rolling hills,
wooded meadows and farmland make up the bucolic
landscape.

A stop is made at Bruderndorf to take on
water before making the final climb to the 2655
foot summit. Before reaching this highest point
on the route, you will also pass through the
two Bruderndorf tunnels, after which you will
be treated to a wonderful panoramic view. The
area serves as a watershed for both the Danube
and Elbe rivers. The remainder of the trip to
Gross Gerungs (2042 feet elev.) is mostly
downhill.

The steam trains run on Fridays, Saturdays
and Sundays, from about May 1 until the end of
September. Departures from Gmund are at 0856
and 1335, and from Gross Gerungs at 1110, 1540
and 1635. The trip in each direction takes one
hour and fifty minutes. There are both 1st and
2nd class accomodations and the fares for each
are as follows: Adult one-way, 90 S 1st class,
60 S 2nd class, round trip, 148 S 1st class, 98
S 2nd class. Children go for a reduced price.
The schedule for the Waldviertelbahnen is number
84 in the Kursbuch.

The company also runs steam trains over two
other routes: Gmund-Alt Nagelberg-Litschau and
Alt Nagelberg-Heidenreichstein. These, however,
are only for groups and for special events and
must be reserved well in advance.

The make-up of the train usually consists
of a steam locomotive, one or two passenger
cars, bar and buffet cars. Good food and drink
is available on board, including the popular
Weitra Pilsen beer.

For additional information, write to:
Osterreichische Bundesbahnen, Generaldirektion,
A-1010 Wien, Elisabethstrasse 9, Austria.

YBBSTALBAHN

South of Autoroute E5, between Linz and
Vienna, there is another steam railway, the
Ybbstalbahn, also operated by the OBB. It goes
by the name "Club 598", which is the number of
their 1896 vintage steam locomotive. The
starting point for this 760mm gauge line is in
the town of Waidhofen, located about 18 miles
south of the Amstetten exit.

The relatively long route extends 42.6

miles, from Waidhofen to Kienberg-Gaming, taking in several towns, crossing the Ybbs river several times and providing the rider with an abundance of wonderful scenery. At Gstadt, which is the first stop on the route, a spur line takes off to the village of Ybbsitz, 3.6 miles to the east.

Unlike most of the tourist steam railways in Austria and elsewhere, this one does not have what might be considered a normal schedule for its steam trains. Instead, it conducts five or six excursions during each season that usually include special events: i.e., visits to an important landmark, a hike through the woods, lectures, picnic, etc.

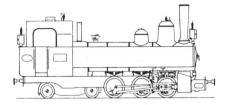

Club 598

The route itself, however, is covered several times daily by the OBB's regular diesel or electric trains, and the trip takes about 2 hours and 20 minutes each way.

The steam train excursions last anywhere from four to eight hours and the fares are in the 90-130 S range for adults, and the 60-80 S range for children 6-13 years old.

The railway was formed in 1895 by the Ybbstalbahn AG, and the initial section between Waidhofen and Hollenstein was completed in July of 1896. By May of 1898, the line had been extended to Lunz am Zee and the final stretch to Kienberg-Gaming was opened on the 11th of December that same year. The spur line from Gstadt to Ybbsitz was inaugurated on September 3, 1899.

In 1928, the line was nationalized and went under the direction of the OBB. In 1973, "Club 598" was formed by the Freunde der Ybbstalbahn to operate tourist steam trains over the line. From the OBB, they purchased steam locomotive # 598.02, the engine that hauled the very first train over the line back in 1896. After 450,000 Shillings and 7,000 hours of labor, the engine was completely restored and, on October 13-14, made its first complete roundtrip of the route.

Upon departing Waidhofen, you travel eastward toward Gstadt, crossing the Ybbs River via the 256-foot long Schwarzbach bridge, on the way out of town. The route follows several valleys as it wends its way, first to the south, then in an easterly direction, to Gostling, before heading north past the Lunzersee toward Gaming. In addition to the six bridges over the Ybbs River, there is also a 285 foot long tunnel at Opponitz.

All of the many towns along the route are interesting enough to make a stop worthwhile and most have well marked scenic walking trails. Also, bikes can be rented from the

railway stations at either Waidhofen or Lunz am
See.

For additional information or a current
schedule, write: Club 598, Hohenstrasse 49,
3340 Waidhofen/Ybbs, Austria.

MARIAZELLERBAHN

Mariazell world premier
exibition of trains/
trams, autos and air-
planes held in May 1987.
(Museumbahn Mariazell-
Erlaufsee).

The Museumbahn Mariazell-Erlaufsee, located
in the town of Mariazell, operates steam trains
twice a month from the first week in June
until the end of october.   The 1-1/2 mile long
standard gauge railway, which was built during
the years 1980-1984, carries passengers between
the Mariazell Bahnhof and the Erlufsee.

Primarily a museum for the preservation of
light railway vehicles (street railway cars and
engines) the museum is the proud owner of the
world's oldest steam tram. The Tramway-Steam-
Maschine, as it is called, was built in 1884 by
Krauss of Linz and is still in regular use.
That is only their main prize, however. They
also have four other steam locomotives and more
than a dozen trams and other utility street
cars. With the exception of a street car
acquired from Branford, New York, most of the
other cars and engines were formerly operated
on the streets of Vienna, Graz, Salzburg and
St. Poltner.

The 25 minute trip begins at the station of
the narrow gauge Mariazellerbahn, about a mile
from Mariazell in the town of St. Sebastian.
Regular stops are made at two small stations
along the heavily wooded route that parallels
the road from Mariazell to Erlufsee.   The
Erlufsee, although rather small, is quite
beautiful and very popular.

Route of the Maria-
zellerbahn and also
the side-trip to
burgeralp via
the Gondolabahn.
(Museumbahn Mariazell-
Erlaufsee).

For a really wonderful full-day outing, you
might try the following. Start the day by
taking the Gondolabahn from Mariazell to the
Berghotel on the summit of the 4155 foot high
Burgreralpe. Enjoy a hearty breakfast in the
hotel and then make the scenic hike down to the
Mariazell Bahnhof in St. Sebastian, where you
can catch the Museumbahn to the Erlufsee.
After a leisurly lunch at the Seerestaurant,
followed by a sightseeing trip on the lake, you
are ready for the return trip, via the
Museumbahn, to St. Sebastian. A short trip by
bus and you are back in Mariazell.

During its period of operation, the train
generally makes seven trips per day on at
least one Sunday each month, plus an
occasional Saturday and Monday. Departure
from the Mariazell Bahnhof is on the half hour,

starting at 0930, and from the Erlaufsee on the hour, starting at 1000.

Fares for the Museumbahn only are: Adults, one-way 30 S, round trip 50 S;. Children, 10 S each way. Special group trips can be arranged if reservations are made well in advance.

A combination ticket for the Gondolabahn, Museumbahn and the ship, can be purchased at the tourist bureau in Mariazell.

For additional information, write: Verkehrs-verein Mariazell, A-8630 Mariazell, Hauptplatz 13, Austria.

MUSEUMEISENBAHN PAYERBACH-REICHENAU-HIRSCHWANG

Southwest of Puchberg, and not too far as the crow flies, you will find the Museumeisenbahn Payerbach-Reichenau-Hirschwang. Under the management of the "Osterreichische Gesellschaft fur Lokalbahnen (OGLB)," the steam driven "Hollental Express" carries passengers along 3.1 miles of 760 mm gauge track.

Starting from the Payerbach-ort station, the route climbs gradually up a wooded slope to Artzberg, the highest point on the line at 1693 feet, and then descends into the Schwarza valley to Kurhaus. After departing Kurhaus, which is 1.2 miles into the route, the tracks make a nearly complete circle (the Thalhof Loop) followed by a sharp reverse curve, before crossing the Kurhaus bridge. The 102-foot long, 19-foot high, bridge which crosses the Vienna aqueduct is the railway's largest engineering work. From there, the line runs along a low enbankment on the floor of the valley and into the Reichenau station at 1.6 miles. The town itself, which is across the river, can be reached via a bridge directly from the station. An electrical sub-station at Reichenau transforms high voltage AC current to 500 volt DC for the company's electric locomotives.

Continuing along the floor of the valley, past gardens and meadows, you come to Haaberg, 2.6 miles into the route and the last stop before the end of the line. The final half mile takes you closer and closer to the river before reaching the Hirschwang station at the foot of the Mittagstein.

The route is very scenic, with woods on both sides for nearly the entire distance and snow-capped moutains in view much of the time.

The railway was built in 1917 to carry supplies for the construction of a standard gauge line and also to carry goods to a pulpmill in Hirschwang. After the fall of the Austro-

Hungarian Empire in 1918, the work on the standard gauge railway was suspended and the pulpmill sold.

In 1922, the Lokalbahn-Payerbach-Hirschwang AG (LBP-H) was formed to convert the industrial railway into a public railway for passenger service. Between the years 1927 and 1963, the railway also had a branch that ran to the Rax Funicular and another branch connecting Payerbach and Payerbach-Lokalbanh. Due in large part to the increase in the number of automobiles, passenger service on the line was discontinued on July 1, 1963. The two branch lines were abandoned at approximately the same time. Freight traffic, which had been seriously cut back over the years, ended on August 11, 1982.

The O.G.L.B. was founded in 1977 to preserve the history of the local railway and to resume passenger service using steam, diesel and electric locomotives--a service unique in Austria. Through the efforts of the members of the association who not only contributed money but worked many hours without pay, the tracks and the overhead lines were repaired, many cars were restored, and engines rebuilt. Additional cars and engines were purchased from other defunct lines and, within the short span of two years, the Hollental-Express began operation in the summer of 1979.

Their rolling stock consists of: two electric locos, (E1 and E2) both built in 1903; one diesel loco built in 1925; two steam locos, (#298.51 "U1 NOLB" and "Floriana"); a variety of vintage passenger coaches; and assorted service vehicles.

The trains run mostly on Sundays, but they also run on various other days, especially holidays, so it is advisable to send for a current schedule before making a special trip to the area.

Departure times from Payerbach-Ort station are 0910, 1045, 1210, 1445, 1645, and 1845, and the trip takes just about 25 minutes including the three intermediate stops. Trains leave Hirschwang at 0830, 1000, 1130, 1400, 1600 and 1800. Usually twice a year (in 1987, July 4 and August 29), they have what is called "Steam in the Moonlight," which includes a 3 hour long bar-b-que at Reichenau, before returning to Payerbach in the moonlight. For those who aspire to be engineers, it is also possible to drive the locomotive, however, the price might be considered a little high at 500 S for one hour, or 900 S for 2 hours. In addition to all the foregoing, the train is also available for group charter.

The engine and cars of the narrow gauge Feist-ritzbahn crossing one of several bridges along its route. The 14.5 mile trip takes just over one hour. (Steiermärkische Landes-bahnen).

Three engines belonging to the Landesbahn Unzmarkt-Tamsweg (Murtalbahn). The railway provides both diesel and steam-powered trains on their routes through the beautiful countryside. (Landesbahn Unzmarkt-Tamsweg).

Engine #671 of the Graz-Koflacher Eisenbahn is one of the oldest running steam locomotives in the world. Built in 1860, it is still in use on this, Austria's largest private railway. (Fotoverlag Reinhold Jungels).

Adult fares for the trip between Payerbach and Hirschwang are: one-way 30 S, round trip 50 S., Children (6-15) years and seniors, pay half price. For group fares or the moonlight ride, write for current fares. Osterreichische Gesellschaft fur Lokalbahnen, Postfach 625, 1150 Vienna Austria.

Payerbach can be reached by the OBB or by bus/auto via Autoroute (A2) or highway (S6).

FEISTRITZTALBAHN

Another steam train, the Feistritztalbahn, joins the towns of Weiz and Birkfeld, both of which are located on secondary route 72 about 30 miles northwest of Graz. The line is owned by the Steiermarkische Landesbahnen which operates diesel powered trains over the route all year round.

The steam trains run on Wednesdays, Thursdays and Saturdays, beginning about the first week of July and continuing until about the middle of September. There are usually two trains each day. For special events or group trips, arrangements can be made for other than the scheduled days and times.

There is also a "Hobby Zug" or "Amateur Lok," as it is sometimes called, which can be chartered by individuals or groups.

Between Birkfeld and Weis, the 14.5 mile route of the narrow gauge (760mm) line passes through some ruggedly beautiful scenery, crossing the Feistritz River three or four times via picturesque viaducts and bridges. The trip, which takes just over one hour, includes stops at five small towns along the way.

In addition to the company's several diesel and electric engines and a large number of passenger and freight cars for their regular service, they also have two steam locomotives and four or five vintage coaches. The steam locomotives were built in 1922 and 1926.

For additional information, write: Steiermarkische Landesbahnen, Radetzkystrasse 31 8010 Graz, Austria.

GRAZ-KOFLACHER EISENBAHN

Graz, Austria's second largest city, is the headquarters of the standard gauge, Graz-Koflacher Eisenbahn (GKB), the country's largest private railway. The GKB offers steam train excursions over two different routes. The first

one starts at the Graz koflacher Bahnhhof in
Graz and takes you south to Leibock, then
northwest to Koflach, a distance of 24.5 miles.
The second route, which begins at Koflach,
travels 30.6 miles, in a mostly southerly
direction, to the town of Wies-Eibiswald. Both
routes pass through scenic, rural agricultural
countryside, and include stops at several small
towns along the way.

Although the routes are traveled several
times daily by diesel driven trains, the steam
trains run only during the summer. The season
starts in mid-June with a three-day exibition
of railway equipment, model trains and steam
engines, and continues into August. Several
special excursions are scheduled for each year;
two of which last between 9 and 12 hours.

The railway's rolling stock includes: steam
locomotives #50.1171, built in Czechoslovakia
in 1942; #56.3115, a 1914 Austrian engine: and
#671, one of the oldest running steam
locomotives in the world, built in 1860. They
also have six diesel engines, three diesel
railcars (combination engine and passenger car)
and numerous passenger coaches, some of which
are genuine museum pieces.

Since the season's starting date and
schedule changes each year, it is advisable to
write in advance for current fares and
schedules. Write to GKB-Reisburo, Grazbachgasse
39, 8010 Graz, Austria.

MURTALBAHN

Marau, named for the river Mur on whose
banks it lies, is the headquarters for the
Murtalbahn, a combination steam and diesel-
powered narrow gauge railway.

With Murau as the dividing point, the steam
driven trains make the 23 mile trip up the
valley to Tamsweg and the trains making the 16
mile trip down to Uzmarkt, are pulled by diesel
powered locomotives. The entire 39 mile route
of the Murtalbahn is one of exceptional charm,
but, unfortunately, most people never make it
past the steam section.

Except for special group excursions at
other times, the two sections operate from
about July 10 until September 4, carrying both
passengers and freight. Besides the regularly
scheduled steam trains to and from Tamsweg, the
railway runs a "slow train" for the benefit of
rail fans who delight in endless photo taking.
There is also a "hobby or amateur train" where
it is possible to actually drive the train

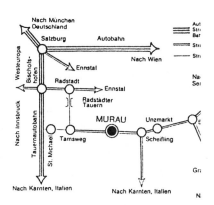

and   become a "certified locomotive engineer".

The "slow train" from Murau to Tamsweg takes appoximately 1 hour and 35 minutes, including stops at St. Lorenzen ob Murau, Stadl-Kaltwasser and Ramingstein-Thomatal. This is about 10 or 15 minutes longer than the regular trip. The round trip fare is 140 Shillings, and, because of the lengthy layover at each end, many passengers choose to take a bus back to their starting point instead of waiting.

The "hobby" train makes one hour runs only and the cost is considerably higher.

The route of the Murtalbahn is within sight of the Mur river for nearly its whole length and presents a great variety of pleasing scenery. There are a number of bridges, tunnels and stone viaducts along the way to be enjoyed as you move from town to town through the Austrian countryside.

The 760mm gauge line is nearing its one hundredth year, having been completed and put into service on October 9, 1894.

For additional information, write: Landesbahn Unzmarkt-Tamsweg (Murtalbahn), 8850 Marau, Austria.

The Stainzerbahn's steam locomotive # U8 pulling the Stainzer Flascherlzug. The line boasts seven steam locomotives in all, plus three diesel engines. (Club 760, photo: H.Gullich).

STAINZERBAHN

About 10 or 15 miles southwest of Graz, on route 76, you will come to the town of Stainz, which is the northern railhead of the Stainzerbahn. Originally part of the GKB, the route of the Stainzerbahn, which is between Stains and Preding-Wieselsdorf, was opened in 1892.

Steam train service over the 6.7 mile long narrow gauge (760mm) line, which is operated by an association known as Club 760, is from the beginning of May to the end of October. Departures from Stainz are as follows: from the beginning of May to the end of June, at 1500 hours every Friday, Saturday and Sunday; July 1 to the end of August, every Friday and Sunday at 1500; and from September 1 to the end of October, every Friday and Saturday at 1000. The trip takes approximately 45 minutes each way, including stops at Herbersdorf and Neudorf. There is a 1/2 hour layover in Preding-W., which is enough time for a little sightseeing or a bite to eat. The route is similar to that of the GKB in that the scenery is largely an agricultural landscape, with wooded hills in the near distance.

The steam train goes by the name "Flascherlzug" and usually consists of steam locomotive S 11 "Stainz" pulling four or five passenger coaches, each with a different color and name. The blue car is Bi31, "Schilcherschaukel;" Red is Bi32, "Bergliesl;" Green is Bi33, "Hollerhansl;" Yellow Bi 34, Krauterwagerl;" and Cream/Brown Bi37, "Stadt Tamsweg."

Fares for the Flascherlzug are 80 S for adults and 40 S for children (6-15). The fares are for one-way, or round trip.

They also have a "Hobby Zug" which goes for 2000 S per hour and also group trips at other than regular times if reserved in advance.

Their rolling stock includes: seven steam locomotives built between 1892 and 1916; three diesel engines from the 1940's; six passenger cars from the 1970's and 80's (all but one, are from the OBB); and a variety of other railcars.

For additional information, write: Marktgemeinde Stainz "Club 760" 8510 Stainz, Austria.

GURKTALBAHN

Still farther south and west, the Karntner Museumbahnen of Klagenfurt, Austria's oldest museumbahnen, also operates steam trains over a short, but picturesque, route.

The narrow gauge (760mm) Gurktalbahn which was established in 1974, carries passengers between the villages of Pockstein/Zwischen-wassern and Krumfelden, a distance of 1.20 miles.

South of Klagenfurt, near the Yugoslavian border, the museum also operates the Rosentaler Dampfzuge over the standard gauge tracks of the OBB. This 12-mile route, Rosenbach-Wizeldorf-Ferlach, is usually run only once or twice a year, in July and August.

The narrow gauge Gurktal-bahn of the Karntner museum-bahnen, Austria's oldest museum railway.
(Karntner Museumbahnen)

Special trips and a "hobby train" are also available when reservations are made in advance.

The Gurktalbahn, powered by steam locomotives "Anny," "Uta" or "Christl," runs every Saturday and Sunday, from the third week in June to the middle of September. On Saturdays, departures from Pockstein/Z are at 1400 and 1600. On Sundays, there are two additional departures at 1000 and 1200. Departures from Krumfelden are 1045, 1245, etc.

The round trip fare for adults is 40 S and for children (1-15), 20 S.

The usual makeup of the train behind the engine is two or three open platform coaches, a buffet car and baggage car (used as a souvenir and information car). The train crew is most obliging when it comes to making photo stops and, of course, knows the best places to get unusual pictures.

The Museum has on exhibit more than a dozen steam locomotives, several diesels, and many passenger and other cars and memorabilia.

For additional information or current dates for either of the routes, write: Karntner Museumbahnen, A-9010 Klagefurt, Postfach 321, Austria.

(Above) Engine # B 1266 of the Angelner Dampfeisenbahn. Built in 1915
for the Schwedischen Staatseisenbahn, it has a top speed of 54 MPH.
(Angelner Dampfeisenbahn)

(Below) Preparing for departure is the 1899 vintage steam locomotive "Hoya"
of the Deutscher Eisenbahn Verein e.V., Germany's first museum railway.
(Eberhard Kunst)

G E R M A N STEAM RAILWAYS

1	ANGELNER DAMPFEISENBAHN
2	MUSEUMBAHN am SCHONBERGER STRAND
3	DEUTSCHER EISENBAHN VEREIN e.V.
4	VEREIN BRAUNSCHWEIGER VERKEHRSFREUNDE e. V.
5	DAMPFEISENBAHN WESERBERGLAND
6	MINDENER KREISBAHNEN
7	WITTLLAGER KREISBAHN
8	VORWOHLE-EMMENTHALER EISENBAHN
9	VOLDAGSEN-SALZHEMMENDORF DUINGEN EISENBAHN
10	KREIENSEN-KALEFELD EISENBAHN
11	DAMPF-KLEINBAHN MUHLENSTROTH
12	KRENFELDER EISENBAHN
13	SELFKANTBAHN
14	HESSENCOURRIER
15	EISENBAHNMUSEUM BOCHUM-DAHLHAUSEN
16	DEUTSCHES MUSEUMS-EISENBAHN
17	JAGSTTALBAHN
18	DAMPF 85
19	ALBTALBAHN
20	BAHNLINE AMSTETTEN-GERSTETTEN
21	**EISENBAHNFREUNDE ZOLLERNBAHN**
22	KAISERSTUHL-DAMPFZUG "REBENBUMMLER"
23	MUSEUMBAHN WUTACHTAL
24	MUSEUMBAHN OCHSENHAUSEN-WARTHAUSEN
25	**BAYERISCHER LOCALBAHN VEREIN e. V.**
26	CHIEMSEE-BAHN

CHAPTER SIX

GERMAN STEAM RAILWAYS

The German people seem to have a genuine love for the railways of yesterday, but they have a particular fondness for steam locomotives. Associations of railway enthusiasts all over Germany have labored long and hard, and spent millions of dollars to preserve the history of steam railways. The large number of railway museums and "Museumbahns" scattered throughout the country are proof of their success.

Most but, unfortunately, not all of the existing steam railway lines in Germany are described in the following pages.

ANGELNER DAMPFEIFENBAHN

The northernmost of Germany's steam railways is the Angelner Dampfeifenbahn. Established in 1977 with the acquisition of their first steam locomotive, the ten-mile long railway operates entirely with Scandinavian rolling stock.

Maintained and supported mostly by volunteers, their rolling stock has grown to include: two steam locomotives, engine # F654 built in 1947 and formerly of the Danischen Staatsbahnen (DSB); engine #1266 from 1915, formerly of the Schwedischen Staatseisnbahn (SJ); one diesel motorcar, # MO 1839 also formerly of the (DSB); two passenger coaches from the Norwegischen Staatsbahnen (NSB); and some other coaches and assorted rail cars from all three lines.

Service is during the summer only, from

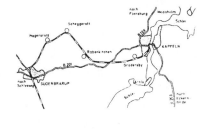

May through September, generally on two Sundays a month, with three round trips being made on each of the "train days." The first departure from Kappeln is at 1030 and the last returning train leaves Suderbrarup at 1720.

The train also makes special trips through Easter week and features a "Santa Claus" train during December.

Starting from the town of Kappeln, located on an inlet of the Ostsee (Baltic Sea), the route wends its way eastward for ten miles to Suderbrarup. With four regular stops along the way, not including a possible photo stop, the trip will take at least forty minutes. A round trip from Kappeln, with a thirty minute layover in Suderbrarup, requires approximately two hours.

The dates and times for all of the trains, including the special ones, are subject to change from year to year. For additional information or a current schedule of dates and fares, write: Freunde des Schienenverkehrs, Postfach 1617, 2390 Flensburg, Germany.

MUSEUMBAHN am SCHONBERGER STRAND

Also located in the far north of Germany near Kiel is another steam train that operates between the village of Schonberg and Schonberg Strand, on the shore of the Ostsee. The railway, the Verein Verkehrsamateure and Museumsbahn (VM), is what is left of a railway line established in 1914 that connected Schonberg with Kiel. Unfortunately, this 2.5 mile stretch, which was the last section of the once 12.5 mile long line to be built, is now the only section still in use. Regular train service on the Kiel/Schonberg route ended in 1975 for lack of passengers. In 1976, limited service over this much reduced portion of the route was resumed under the present organization. The schedule for this line is 135 in the DB Kursbuch.

The little standard gauge railway has two or three steam locomotives, at least one diesel engine, and several passenger, baggage and miscellaneous other vintage cars.

The train makes frequent trips every Thursday, Saturday and Sunday, from mid-May until mid-September. The one-way and round trip fares for adults and children are: 2.40 and 4.80 DM; and 1.40 and 2.80 DM.

The 15 minute trip is pleasant and the view from Schonberg Strand is really beautiful. There are walking paths along the beach and also back to Schonberg.

For additional information, write: Verein Verkehrsamateure und Museumbahn e. V., Hans J. Kampf, Billhorner Deich 79, 2000 Hamburg 28 Germany.

DEUTSCHER EISENBAHN VEREIN e.V.

To the Deutscher Eisenbahn Verein e. V. (DEV) goes the honor of having founded the first museum railway in Germany. Located south of Bremen, also in the northern part of the country, its 4.7 mile long narrow gauge (1000 mm) line connects the towns of Bruchhausen-Vilsen and Asendorf.

The DEV was formed in 1964 by a group of railway enthusiasts for the purpose of establishing a museum and railway. In 1966 the Hoya County Transport Services (VGH), which had just discontinued freight service on their Bruchhausen-Vilsen-Asendorf route, offered the route to the DEV. In addition to the use of the tracks, they gave to the DEV the steam locomotive "Bruchhausen" which the DEV had just recently tried to buy from them.

On July 2 1966, the "Bruchhausen," pulling coach # 0140 (purchased from the DB's narrow gauge Mosbach-Mudau/Odenwald line) departed from the Bruchhausen-Vilsen station and began its inaugural trip to Heligenberg.

By the end of the year the DEV had acquired eight more pieces of equipment and had carried an average of 200 pasengers per trip during its five operating days.

In 1967 the VGH made available a second steam engine, # 3341 "Hoya" (an 0-6-0 tank engine) built by Hanomag in 1899.

In 1969 the remaining section of the route from Heligenberg to Asendorf was put into service, bringing the line's length to the present 4.7 miles. In the months and years to follow, all of the stations were reconstructed, the maintenance and exhibition shed in Bruchhausen-vilsen was built, rolling stock was added, and numerous other buildings repaired or constructed.

The railway is operated entirely by its members, and every volunteer is trained for the job he does and has to pass an appropriate examination before starting his job.

On each Sunday and holiday from the beginning of May to the end of September and on each Saturday during July, August and September, three trips are made in each direction. On Saturdays the first train leaves Bruchhausen V.

at 1000. The sunday and holiday departures begin at 1400. The schedule is # 114 in the DB Kursbuch. The adult one-way fare is 8.40 DM.

The scenic 38-minute ride from Bruchhausen-Vilsen to Asendorf includes wooded areas, meadows, farmhouses, and even a millpond complete with a waterwheel. Passengers have several opportunities for picture taking as the trip includes station stops in the towns of Heligenberg and Wiehe Kurpark.

The line also runs several special trains including the "Father-Christmas-Specials" in December, the night-time "Count of Bruchhausen" train in September, "Railfans' Day" trains, and special group train excursions that can be arranged for other than the regular dates and times.

Their extensive roster of equipment includes: four steam locomotives; two diesel engines; four railcars; eight passenger coaches; two baggage cars; one buffet car; and fifty freight cars.

The four steam locomotives are: the "Franzburg," 1894 by Vulcan; "Hoya," 1899 by Hanomag; "Hermann," 1911 by Hohenzollern; and "Spreewald," 1917 by Jung. The two diesel locomotives were built by Krupp and Deutz and are from 1941 and 1954 respectively. All but one of the coaches are from the turn of the century.

For additional information regarding schedules or fares, write: Deutscher Eisenbahn Verein e. V., Postfach 1106, D-2814 Bruchhausen-Vilsen, Germany.

VEREIN BRAUNSCHWEIGER VERKEHRSFREUNDE e. V.

The (BLME) Braunschweigesche Landes-Museum-Eisenbahn, which is owned and operated by the association Verein Braunschweiger Verkehrs-freunde e.V. (VBV), runs steam and diesel powered trains over a group of routes north of Braunschweig. The original railway line here dates back to 1895, but it was taken over by the VBV sometime after 1949 for the operation of tourist trains.

There are two separate trains involved here: the Preussenzug, which is the steam train; and the Celler Land-Express, which is powered by a diesel locomotive. For the most part, the two trains travel different routes through a scenic area of the country known as the Sudheide.

Although the season for the Preussenzug's excursions does not start until June, the VBV

Built in 1912, engine # 1 of the BLME is now out of service. (BLME)

(Above) Built in 1925, locomotive # 6, "Hohenzollern," is seen pulling the "Prusssenzug" on
one of its several routes in a northeastern part of Germany known as the Sudheide. (BLME)

(Below) The standard gauge engine "Stettin 7906" of the Mindener Kreisbahnen
ready to depart the Bohmte station with its five vintage coaches. (Ingrid Schutte)

has events going on all-year long. There are
outings on trains of the DB, rides on city
trams, films, harvest festivals, and workshops.

The schedule varies some each year, but
generally, the steam trains operate on one or
two Sundays a month until September, with the
first train of the day departing at 1000.

One route takes you from the town of
Hankensbuttel to Brome, a distance of about 18
miles. The trip, which is made three times
during the season, takes you through a partially
wooded region along the East German border. In
August, the same train makes at least one round
trip between Steinhorst and Brome via Wittingen
and Hankensbuttel, a 48-mile trip. Later, in
September, a trip is made from Brome to Parsau
for the celebration of the "Erntefest" or
harvest festival. The trips range in length from
about an hour to just under two hours in each
direction, but, due to a very long layover at
each destination, the outing takes most of the
day. There are so many interesting sights to
see and things to do at each place, however,
most passengers are happy for the extra time.

The Celler Land-Express, using diesel
power, departs from Celle and goes north to
Muden/Ortze (19 miles) and also to Wittingen
via Hankensbutel (29 miles). On the stretch
between Hankensbuttel and Wittengen, the steam
locomotive "Hohenzollern" is substituted for the
diesel engine. Also between Hankensbuttel and
Wittengen, the route crosses the Elbe
Seitenkanal, which, under several different
names, flows from the Baltic Sea to the North
Sea.

The rolling stock of the Prussenzug
includes the following: steam locomotive #2,
"Braunschweig," built in 1925; steam locomotive
#6, "Hohenzollern," also from 1925; diesel
locomotive # V36311, built in 1943; passenger
cars "Naumburg," 1897; "Verden," 1886;
"Potsdam," 1878; "Erfurt," 1905; and
"Frankfurt," from 1917. Other equipment
includes a buffet car, baggage car and several
freight cars.

The Celler Land-Express rolling stock
consists of: one 1942 diesel locomotive,
V36225; a 1923 buffet car; and six passenger
cars from the period 1903 to 1940. Just as with
the Prussenzug, each car is named.

The well-restored vintage coaches, with
their wooden seats and old-time atmosphere,
combined with the slow tempo of the ride, make
for a nostalgic trip and a pleasant return to
days gone by.

Adult one-way and round trip fares for the
Prussenzug are as follows: Hankensbuttel/Brome,

12-18 DM; Steinhorst/Brome, 16-24 DM; Hankens-
buttel/Parsau, 16-24 DM. Children (4-14) travel
for half-price.

Fares from Celle to Muden/Ortze and Celle
to Wittingen via the Celler land-Express are 10-
15 DM, and 11-16 DM respectively.

Both trains offer group trips and fares,
plus special family tickets.

For additional information or current
schedules, write: Verein Braunschweiger,
Verkehrsfreunde e. V., Postfach 5323, 3300
Braunschweig, Germany.

DAMPFEISENBAHN WESERBERGLAND

About 25 miles west of Hanover on highway
B65, in the town of Stadthagen, you will find
the northern terminus of the standard gauge
steam railway, Dampfeisenbahn Weserbergland
(DEW). Operating on the first and third Sundays
of each month from May to October, the steam
train carries tourists and rail fans between
Stadthagen and Rinteln.

Upon leaving Stadthagen, the scenery that
unfolds is mostly a rural landscape, with
picturesque farming country stretching for a
distance of about twelve miles before reaching
Rinteln. With stops at five interesting villages
along the route, plus an occasional "photo
halt", there are plenty of opportunities for
getting great pictures.

The first train leaves from Rinteln at
0940, arriving at Stadthagen at 1040. After a
35 minute layover, it departs Stadthagen at
1115 for the return trip. The second departure
from Rinteln is at 1400, returning there at
1635. There is sometimes a third round trip
which departs from Rinteln at 1800.

The round trip fare is 10 DM for adults
and half-price for children under 14. Special
rates are available for groups of 20 or more
persons, but reservations must be made at least
two weeks in advance.

In existance only since 1972, the line is
the proud owner of five steam locomotives, at
least two diesel engines, a buffet car, and
several old passenger cars.

For additional information, write:
Dampfeisenbahn Weserbergland e. V., Postfach
1211, 3064 Bad Eilsen, Germany.

MINDENER KREISBAHNEN

Approximately 12 miles west of Stadthagen on Rt 65 is the town of Minden, and the headquarters of the Museum-Eisenbahn Minden e.V. With four steam locomotives and several passenger cars, the MEM carries passengers on three different routes over nearly 36 miles of standard gauge track.

The Mindener Kreisbahnen (MKB), pulled by either of two steam locomotives, "Stettin #7906" or "Mevissen #4", makes trips in two directions from the town of Minden. The trains run on the second Sunday of each month, from April to October, one route going northwest to the town of Hille, and the other southeast to Nammen-Grube. The longer of the two is the Minden/Hille route, which is approximately 8 miles long and takes 1 hour and 40 minutes for a round trip. The route between Minden and Nammen-Grube, being slightly shorter, takes 1 hour and 20 minutes.

There is only one round trip per day to Nammen-Grube, so if you want to ride the entire route, you must be there on time for the 10:30 departure. There are two afternoon round trips to Hille, which is convenient if you plan to take both trips and wish to spend some time in Minden.

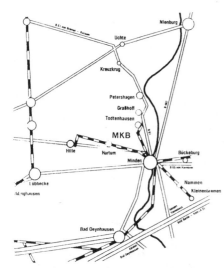

With several villages, nearly a dozen station stops and lots of peaceful rural scenery to enjoy, both trips are really a bargain.

The adult fare for a round trip on each route is 8 DM, or an all-day pass is available for 14 DM. The fare for children (3 to 14) is half of the adult price for either the round trip or the all-day ticket.

WITTLAGER KREISBAHN

The third route run by the MEM originates in the town of Holzhausen-Heddinghausen, a few miles to the west of Minden. The Wittlager Kreisbahn (WKB) operates on the last Sunday of the month, from April to September, between Holzhausen-H. and Schwegermoor, a distance of 23 miles.

Using either locomotive "Alice Heye" or "# 896237," the first train of the day leaves from Preuss Oldendorf (two miles west of Holzhausen-H.) at 1000. This train goes only to Bohmte, which is 45 minutes short of Schwegermoor, and after a twenty-minute layover, turns around and heads for Holzhausen.

At 1250 the second train departs and, after making anywhere from five to eleven stops along the way, pulls into Schwegermoor at 1455. A 55-minute layover allows time for lunch, sightseeing, picture taking, or just relaxing before the return trip.

A complete round trip, which of course includes the stop over, takes just over five hours and costs 10 DM. The fares for the train are broken down into distances, however: the farther you go, the less it costs per Km. It is apparently a common practice for people to go only part way and then either find another way back, or catch the same train when it comes by on the return trip. The fare for children between 3 and 14 years of age is half of the adult fare.

For more information, write: Museums-Eisenbahn Minden e.V., Postfach 2751, 4950 Minden/Westfalen Germany.

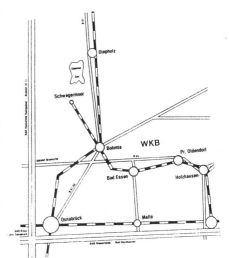

VORWOHLE-EMMENTHALER EISENBAHN

In the region that lies south of Hannover, between the Leine and Wesser rivers, there are three standard gauge steam train routes operated by Dampfzug-Betriebs-Gemeinschaft (DBG).

From Emmenthal, the route of the Vorwohle-Emmenthaler Eisenbahn follows the scenic course of the Wesser river for 8.4 miles before crossing it at Bodenwerder-Kemnade. After the crossing, it continues in a southeasterly direction for another 11.5 miles to the village of Vorwohle.

Service is from the middle of May until mid-October, with one complete round trip and two partial ones each month. The trip takes 1-3/4 hours in each direction, but there is a long lay over at both ends so a round trip takes most of a day. Bicycles and baby carriages are carried free on the train and, since the area is famous for its hiking trails, the extra time could be well spent hiking or bicycling. The adult round trip fare is 19 DM, children ride for 1/2 price. The schedule for this route is # 261 in the DB Kursbuch.

VOLDAGSEN-SALZHEMMENDORF DUINGEN EISENBAHN

The Voldagsen-Salzhemmendorf Duingen Eisenbahn runs a steam train over the second route, between the towns of Voldagsen and Duinen. Operation is usually on the first or second

Sunday of June, July and August. The 9.6 mile route lies to the west, within walking distance of the Thuster and Duniger Bergs, which are very popular with hikers.

Travel time for this trip is approximately one hour each way, with two round trips being made on each operating day. There are several small towns and villages along the route but only three are scheduled stops: Lauenstein, Salzhemmendorf, and Thuste. The adult round trip fare is 9 DM. Children (4-14) pay only 4.5 DM. The schedule for this route is # 263 in the DB Kursbuch.

KREIENSEN-KALEFELD EISENBAHN

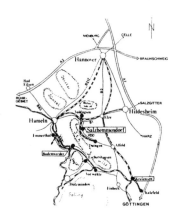

The third route is the 5.4 mile stretch between Kreiensen and Kalefeld, in an area located a few miles north of Gottingen. Like the above two excursions, this one also operates only once a month during a short period each year. In this case the months are August, October, and December. The round trip fare for the 25-minute ride between Kreiensen and Kalefeld is 8 DM for adults and 4 DM for children.

The trains, using vintage steam engines (one from 1928, the other from 1938), pull two or three old-time carriages, a buffet car and bar car. Two regularily scheduled stops and usually one photo stop are made during the trip. The schedule for this route is # 258 in the DB Kursbuch.

For additional information and exact days and times for any particular trip, contact: Dampfzug-Betriebs-Gemeinschaft, Posfach 1422, 3200 Hildesheim 1, Germany.

DAMPF-KLEINBAHN MUHLENSTROTH

Another steam railway, not too far from the one above, is the Dampf-Kleinbahn Muhlenstroth (DKBM), near the town of Gutersloh. If you take autobahn #2 in a southwesterly direction toward Dortmund, you will see the exit to Gutersloh. Go through the town to the north side and look for the sign to the railway on Postdamm Rd.

The narrow gauge (600 mm) railway is located on several acres of farmland surrounding a restaurant. The half-mile layout makes up for its short length with its attractive route through lovely woods and meadows.

One of 5 operating steam locomotives ot the narrow gauge (600mm) Dampf-Kleinbahn Muhlenstroth. Although it is the the shortest line described in this book, it has a very impressive roster of equipment. (Dampf-Kleinbahn Muhlenstroth)

The "Graf Bismark xv," a Henschel built locomotive from 1948, standing at the Hulserberg (also Hulser Berg) station. Nicknamed "der Schluff," this is the only steam engine owned by the standard gauge Krenfelder Eisenbahn. (Foto Studio Martens)

The arrival of Santa Claus for the Selfkantbahn's special Santa Claus Train. This train makes several trips during the month of December each year. (IHS)

The steam trains run every Sunday from the beginnng of May to mid-October and often make as many as 36 trips a day, using two or more steam locomotives. The trip takes six or eight minutes, with trains leaving at approximately the same time from opposite directions, so that they will pass each other at the half way point.

The railway and museum, which was started in 1973, owns 7 steam locomotives (5 running), 5 diesel locomotives (3 running) and two electric engines, both of which are in running condition. They also have 5 closed and 4 open passenger coaches and several miscellaneous freight cars.

The first train is scheduled to depart at 1046 and the last at 1814. The adult fare for the ride is 2.50 DM; Children ride for half-price.

For additional information, write: Dampf-Kleinbahn Muhlenstroth (e.V.), Postdamm 166 4830 Gutersloh, Germany.

KRENFELDER EISENBAHN

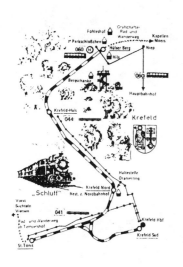

The standard gauge Krenfelder Eisenbahn, operates steam powered trains between the towns of St Tonis and Hulser Berg, which are located just northwest of Dusseldorf.

Pulling four or five cream and red cars, the line's only steam locomotive, Der "Schluff", makes the 8.2 mile trip in approximately one hour. There are only two scheduled stops on the route, Krenfeld Nord and Krenfeld Huls, however, a photo-stop is also generally made somewhere along the way.

Depending on the number of passengers, or whether or not there is a group on board, there is sometimes a saloon car, buffet wagon and/or a bar car. A cook and diskjockey are also available for parties

The steam train runs every Friday and Saturday from the beginning of May to the end of September. Listed as number 479 in the DB Kursbuch, it is scheduled to depart St. Tonis at 1110, 1410, and 1640, and from Hulser Berg at 1230, 1530 and 1800. The adult and children fares for a round trip are: 9.50 DM and 5.00 DM. It is also possible to buy a one-way or round trip ticket for any part of the trip and, with advance reservations, arrangements can be made for special group trips.

The railway was established in 1868 and although it has undergone a great many changes over its more than one hundred years, is still

A four car train of the Hessencourrier crossing a bridge at
Kassel. The locomotive, # T 3
"Walsum," is no longer used
over the route. (Hessencourrier)

One of the several locomotives
owned by the Eisenbahn-museums
Bocum-Dahlhausen heading up a
nine car train. (DGEG)

Shown at a rural crossing near
Blankenbach is engine # 98 727.
Built in 1903, it is formerly of
the Bayerische Staatseisenbahnen.
(DME)

a viable railway. In addition to the steam train, there is regular daily passenger and freight service on the line. The company, at its peak, had as many as 19 locomotives and more than two hundred cars of one kind or another.

Today, its rolling stock is comprised of: one steam locomotive, "Graf Bismarck XV" (der Schluff) built in 1948; four diesel engines, dating from 1954-1975; one diesel rail car; five passenger coaches dating from 1903-1920, one with tables and another with a kitchen; one 1903 vintage bar car; an 1892 baggage car; and two or three other work vehicles.

For additional information, write: Krefelder Verkehrs-AG, St. Toniser Strasse 270, Postfach 1670, 4150 Krefeld, Germany.

SELFKANTBAHN

The Selfkantbahn, operated by the Interess-engemeinschaft Historischer Schienenverkehr e.V. (IHS), runs steam trains on a short stretch of track near Germany's border with Holland.

In 1971 the preservation society took over the remaining 3.3 miles of meter gauge track of the former Geilenkerchener Kreisvahln. The line, which was owned by the communities it served, began service in 1900 and carried both freight and passengers until 1971, the year it ended freight service. Regular passenger service continued over the route until 1960, when it too was discontinued. When the company first started, the 22.8 mile-long route connected the towns of Alsdorf and Tuddern, the former being near Aachen and the latter, adjacent to the Dutch Border. The present route, which is somewhat shorter, connects the towns of Gillrath and Schierwaldenrath.

The steam trains run every Sunday and public holiday from Easter to the end of September and during the four weeks before Christmas. During the Christmas month, each train carries a Santa Claus and operates on both Saturdays and Sundays. There are usually three or four round trips a day starting about 1100 from Schierwaldenrath, or 1200 from Gillrath.

The trip is very scenic, and, with intermediate stops at Gelindchen and Birgden, takes twenty three minutes. The round trip fares are 6.50 DM for adults and 3.50 DM for children. Day tickets can be purchased for 12 DM and 9 DM respectively. The fares for the

Santa Claus trains are slightly higher than for the regular train.

The Selfkantbahn has, in running condition 4 steam engines and about 25 miscellaneous coaches, freight, and other cars, most of which were gathered from various railways, some of which were already extinct. The engines consist of three 040 tender steam locomotives built by Jung in 1956 and a 1930 262 Borsig.

The schedule for this railway is # 458 in the DB Kursbuch. To get to Gillrath, take autobahn A44 to exit Aldenhoven, or A4 to Weisweiler. By train, take the DB to Geilenkirchen, then bus # 35.

For additional information, write: Interessengemeinschaft Historischer Schienenverkehr e.V. (IHS), Postfach 603, 5100 Aachen, Germany.

HESSENCOURRIER

Running through the charming north Hessen Mountain area of eastern Germany, is the line of the Hessencourrier, the areas first museum railway. Started in 1970, the museum's rolling stock includes: a 1952 Henschel steam locomotive, # C206, the last steam locomotive that saw active duty on the old Kleinbahn Kassel-**Naumburg** line; more than two dozen old time coaches (some with open vestibule); a bar car; and a gaslit buffet wagon.

The twenty mile route connects Kassel with **Naumburg,** and the trip, which includes two short stop-overs, takes an hour and forty minutes in each direction. There is a total of six towns along the route and stops are made at all of them, plus a photo stop if requested.

Service is from early May until the middle of October, but the trains usually operate on only one Saturday and one Sunday of each month. Making one round trip per day, they depart from Kassel at either 1000 or 1400, and from **Naumburg** at either 1700 or 1800, depending on the particular day and month. Upon request, special trains for groups can be arranged for nearly any time of the year.

The round trip fare for adults is 20 DM and for children (4-14), 11 DM. A family ticket is available for 50 DM. One way or part way tickets are also available.

For specific information regarding dates and schedules for the time of your visit, write: Hessencourrier e. V., Kaulenbergstrasse 5, 3500 Kassel, Germany.

EISENBAHNMUSEUM BOCHUM-DAHLHAUSEN

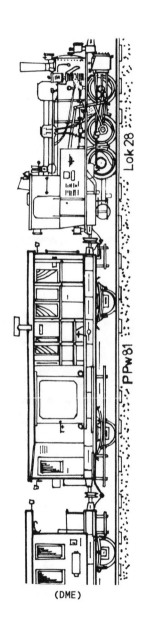

Lok 28

PPw 81

(DME)

Situated northeast of Koln in Bochum-Dahlhausen, is the large and very important Eisenbahnmuseum Bochum-Dahlhausen. The museum, which is owned and operated by the German Society for Railway History, has several steam, diesel and electric locomotives, numerous coaches and an assortment of other railcars. Here you can witness 100 years of living railway history and, during the summer months, ride one of several working trains.

Pulling nine coaches of various design, the museum's trains travel through the beautiful Ruhr valley from Hattingen to Oberwengern, a distance of approximately 13 miles. Stops are made at six towns along the way and every one of them has sights worthy of an extended visit. The route originates in the medieval town of Hattingen, passes through Blankenstein--another ancient town, past the Castle of Blankenstein and the Ruin Hardenstein. Besides being very scenic, the route presents opportunities for several wonderful side trips, especially for hikers. For example, from Blankenstein or Herbede, the second and third stops after departing Hattingen, there are fine foot paths to the Kemnader See where nearly ever kind of water sport is possible. There is also boating on the river, bike paths alongside the river and, from Oberwengern, a good trail leading to the Harkortsee, where there is also water skiing, wind surfing and fishing.

The original railway line here was built in 1874 by an early day railway society, the Bergisch-Markische Eisenbahngesellschaft, and was used primarily for hauling coal from the former Ruhr coal mines. The rails now belong to the DB and, except for the museum trains, are still used for freight traffic.

Excursions for tourists and railway fans are made on the first Sunday of each month, April through October. The schedule may change from time to time, but, at present, the trains make five trips on each of the operating days starting at 0920. With stops at Blankenstein-Burg, Blankenstein-Ruhr, Gerbede, Ruine Hardenstein, Bommern and Wengern Ost, the interesting trip takes just about 45 minutes.

Tickets can be purchased for any part of the trip and are sold on the basis of how many stops you travel. The fare from Hattingen to Oberwengern and return, is 5 DM. Children (4 to 12), go for half-price. All-day tickets and family tickets are also available.

For additional information, write: Eisenbahnmuseum Bochum-Dahlhausen GmbH, Dr.-C.-Otto-
Strasse 191, 4630 Bochum 5, Germany.

DEUTSCHES MUSEUMS-EISENBAHN

The Deutsche Museums-Eisenbahn (DME) in
Darmstadt, was established in 1970 and now has
one of Germany's largest railway collections.
With over 50 historic railway vehicles dating
back to 1887, including several working steam
locomotives, it is truly a living railway
museum. The museum is open every Sunday from
1000 to 1600, plus additional days and hours for
special events. A schedule of those events is
published twice a year and lists, among other
things, exibitions lectures, and train
excursions.

Although secondary to the museum itself,
the rail trips are no doubt very worthwhile.

For additional information and a current
schedule of the steam train's operating dates,
times and fares, write: Duetsche Museums-
Eisenbahn, Steinstrasse 7, 6100 Darmstadt,
Germany.

JAGSTTALBAHN

In the Heilbronn region is Germany's
longest museum railway, a narrow gauge (2feet 5-
1/2 inches) steam railway that offers a ride
that is hard to beat. The Jagsttalbahn,
operated by the Deutsch Gesellschaft Fur
Eisenbahngeschicht e.V., parallels the Jagst
river for 21 miles, crossing it on occasion, as
it travels from Mockmuhl to Dorzbach. The river
which is used for swimming, fishing and boating,
is a very popular family recrearion area.
Canoeing is especially popular and passengers
can arrange to have their canoes carried on the
train. Bicycles are also available for renting
at some stations.

The train's schedule is made up a year in
advance and varies from year to year, but
generally speaking, it runs on one Saturday and
one Sunday of each month, April to October.
Anyone interested in riding on this train would
be well advised to write for a current schedule,
well in advance of going to Europe.

The train stops at most of the many towns
along the route, but generally only long
enough to pick up or let off passengers and
baggage. Several of the stations are starting

points for hiking trips which are also a very popular activity in the area.

At the time of this writing, the one way distances and one way and round trip fares from Mockmuhl are as follows: Widdern (8km) 5/7 DM; Jagsthausen (14km) 7/10 DM; Schontal (21km) 9/13 DM; Westernhausen (26km) 11/13 DM; Krautheim (33km) 13/16 DM; Dorzbach (39km) 14/17 DM. The fares for children 4-12 years of age are half of the adult price.

A complete round trip, Mockmuhl/Dorzbach, takes most of a day, with the travel time alone taking six hours, plus a 2-1/2 hour layover in Dorzbach. The train doesn't go all the way to Dorzbach every time however. On some days it goes only as far as Schontal and return. On the days it stops at Schontal, it makes two round trips. There is time for only one trip on the days it goes all the way to Dorzbach.

To get to Mockmuhl from Heilbronn, take Autobahn 81 and get off at the Mockmuhl exit.

For additional information, write: Deutsche Gesellschaft fur Eisenbahngeschichte e.V. Geschaftsstelle: Postfach 1627, D 7100 Heilbronn, Germany.

DAMPF 85

The year 1985 was the 150th anniversary of the Deutsche Bundesbahn and, to celebrate, the DB sponsored what they called "Dampf 85". Starting in May of that year and continuing through September, they operated steam trains over eight different routes in the Nurnberg area. The trains were scheduled so that each route was run five or six times during the period. In addition, there were several kinds of special-event trips including: outings for school children; photo trips for rail fans; trips for hikers; and even a Santa Claus train, in December of course.

Because of the success of the program, it was followed by "Dampf 86" and "Dampf 87." It's reasonable to assume that there will be a "Dampf 88" etc.

Since the routes, dates, and times have changed each year, it would be advisable to write ahead for current schedules. Deutsche Bundesbahn, "Dampf 8-" Sandstrasse 38-40 8500 Nurnberg, Germany.

The standard gauge Albtalbahn travels the beautiful Alb Valley between the towns of Ettlingen and Bad Herrenalb. The 12-mile trip through the northern Black Forest takes about 45 minutes and includes a number of picturesque station stops. (Bernhardt Hoch)

Engine # 86 345, also of the Albtalbahn, making up a train at the Bad Herrenalb station. (UEF)

ALBTALBAHN

The Albtal Railway, which presently operates a steam train, the Albtalbahn, between Ettlingen and Bad Herrenalb, was built during the years 1897 to 1901. As a meter gauge line, it ran both steam and electric trains over the route until 1957. In that year, due to the very poor condition of its tracks and rolling stock, it was taken over by the newly founded "Albtal-Traffic-Society," which relaid the tracks to standard gauge, bought 25 new tramcars and extended the line into the heart of Karlsruhe. Today the Albtal Railway is a modern and attractive suburban railway system connecting the southern and northern regions around Karlsruhe.

Starting from Ettlingen, which is the beginning of the Alb Valley, the steam train follows the valley floor to Etzenrot and Marxzell (the location of the railway museum). From there it continues on, past the historic nunnery at Frauenalb, to the town of Bad Herrenalb (a thermal spa at the hub of seven valleys). The route takes you through the Northern Black Forest, which, with its many good hotels and restaurants, is a very popular holiday retreat. Less than ten minutes after you depart Ettlingen, you cross the Alb river and arrive at your first stop, Waldbronn-Busenbach. The town is best known as a health resort, having several thermal spas, and is also the rail junction to Ittersbach via the Otschaften Reichenbach.

After making a very short stop at Etzenrot and passing the flag stop at Fischweier, you arrive at Marxzell, the site of the rail museum. From Marxzell it is only a ten minute ride to Frauenalb-Schielberg and another eight minutes to your destination at Bad Herrenalb. The extremely scenic 12 mile trip, with its several station stops, is made in 46 minutes.

The steam trains generally operate on the last Saturday and Sunday of each month from May through October. On Saturdays it departs from Ettlingen at 1432 and from Bad Herrenalb (for the return trip) at 1730. On Sundays there are two trips. Departure times from Ettlingen are 1032 and 1432 and from Bad Herrenalb, 1230 and 1630. One-way fares are: adults, 5.- DM; children, 2.5 DM.

There are also special group trips and an occasional photo trip to Bad Herenalb, using engines #01 509 and #58 311, and to Ittersbach with engine #58 311. In December, the train also makes several "Nikolaus" trips with Santa riding on the train.

A four car train of the Bahnline Amstetten-Gerstetten waits at the station. The engine, # 98 812, previously served both the Bayerische Lokalbahn and the Association Ulmer Eisenbahnfreunde. (Ulmer Eisenbahnfreunde e.V.)

A beautiful winter scene greets riders of the steam train Zollernbahn. The line operates steam trains over seven different routes in the southern part of Germany. (Eisenbahnfreunde Zollernbahn e. V.)

The Albtalbahn is operated by the Ulmer Eisenbahnfreunde, which was organized in 1971 to encourage the preservation of railway history and to operate the steam railway and museum.

Although the line's rolling stock includes five steam locomotives, not all of them are available for use on the Albtalbahn. They are so popular that one or more of them are usually out on loan. The locomotives are: # 58 311, a Prussian G 12 engine; #86 346, a DRG built tank engine; # 01 1066, a DRG built fast train engine; # 01 509, another DRG built engine "Pacific;" #75 1118, a tank engine formerly of the "Badische Staatsbahn."

They also have six coaches. Five are seat-coaches and one is a club-coach and all are former DRG-semi-fast-train coaches built between 1935 and 1938. Another seat-coach is in the process of being rebuilt into a restaurant-car.

For additional information regarding current schedules of dates and times, write: Albtal-Verkehrs-Gesellschaft MbH, Kaiserallee 17a, D-7500 Karlsruhe 1, Germany

BAHNLINE AMSTETTEN-GERSTETTEN

Heading north from Ulm on highway B10, you will come to the town of Amstetten, which is the starting point of the Bahnline Amstetten-Gerstetten. On every second Saturday from May to mid-October, the steam train operated by the Ulmer Eisenbahnfreund makes excursions over the 6 1/2 miles of standard gauge track between Amstetten and Gerstetten. A 1911 locomotive, # 98812, generally pulls two passenger coaches (dating from the years 1928 and 1929), a 1901 baggage car, and one or more other vintage passenger coaches, if needed.

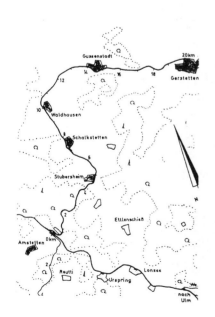

The route between Amstetten and the first stop at Stubersheim is all up hill and accounts for a change in elevation of 333 feet. Shortly after leaving Stubersheim you start a very gradual descent, making stops at Schalkstetten, Waldhausen, Gussenstadt and Siedlung before reaching Gerstetten. At Schalkstetten the train takes on water, which is a perfect situation for taking photos of both the train and the surrounding scenery. At Gestetten there is another water tower which may be ascended to view the surrounding area.

The trip takes approximately 45 minutes and the round trip fares are: 11 DM for adults; and 5 DM for children. Special trains for groups can be chartered for any time of the year providing arrangements are made well in

Shown at left is the Kaiserstuhlbahn, better-known as the "Rebenbummler." The nickname, which when translated means "vineyard stroller," comes from the fact that its route circumvents a a volcanic mountain surrounded by vineyards. (Eisenbahnfreunde Breisgau e. V: Photo by K.H. Sprich).

The 15.6 mile route of the Museumsbahn Wutachtal through the magnificient Wutachtal Valley, is one of the most scenic in all of Germany. With hardly a straight stretch of track on the entire route, it wends its way between the towns of Blumberg and Weizen. (Museumsbahn Wutachtal)

Two steam trains of the narrow gauge (750mm) Museumsbahn Warthausen-Ochsenhausen at the Maselheim station. Shown in the photo is one of the line's 8 steam locomotives. (Schumacher)

advance. The regular schedule for this line is # 906 in the Kursbuch.

For additional information, write: Burgermeisteramt Amstetten, Lonetalstrasse 3A, 7341 Amstetten, Germany.

EISENBAHNFREUNDE ZOLLERNBAHN

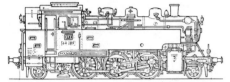
© R. Stöckle, Augsburg

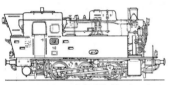
© R. Stöckle, Augsburg

The Eisenbahnfreunde **Zollernbahn** (EFZ), also standard gauge, operates steam trains over seven different routes in the southern part of Germany. The area covered by the routes includes among other things, the Nekar, Danube, Schmiecha and Laucher rivers, and is one of exceptional beauty.

The schedule is made up a year in advance with the trains traveling on specific routes on various Sundays and Wednesdays from May to October. The routes range in length from 4.8 miles to about 30 miles, and, timewise, from 30 minutes to nearly two hours each way.

The following routes, with one exception, are all located southwest of Stuttgart on or near highways 313 or B27.

Route 1: Gammertingen to Kleinengstingen. Nineteen trips are made on this route over a period of six days between June 1 and October 5. The 20 Km stretch is covered in 40 minutes, allowing for five station stops along the route. After a 20 minute layover, the train returns to Gammertingen. The first train usually departs from Gammertingen at 0940.

Route 2: Three trips are made daily over the Bad Friedrichall-Jagstfeld-Ohrnberg route but only on two days in August of each year. The 23 Km long trip with its nine intermediate stops takes approximately 55 minutes. Bad Friedrichshall is located just north of Heilbronn, on highway B27, and can be reached by taking the Neuenstadt exit off the Wurzzburg-Stuttgart autobahn.

Route 3: The Kleinengstingen-Sigmaringdorf route is known as "Wander Bummelzug" because it is used only as a special train for hikers. Operated only during the month of July, it goes via Gammertingen and makes four trips as far as Gammertingen, but only two of them go on to Sigmaringdorf. The distance to Sigmaringdorf is 50Km, and the time required for the trip is 1 hour and 45 minutes. There are nine stops on this route also. The first steam train departs Kleinengstingen at 0745.

Route 4: The Hechingen-Kleinengstingen route. Another Wander Bummelzug, it runs only in October. Going via Gammertingen, the 47 Km long route, with 14 stations en route, takes 1 hour and 55 minutes each way. From the vicinity of Kleinengstingen, hikers go to the "Castle Lechtenstein" and the "bear dens." From Hechingen, the walks are generally to the "Burg Hohenzollern." There is also bus service to these places for those who prefer not to walk.

Route 5: Kleinengstingen-Neufra/Hettingen. This is the same train as above. It makes one round trip between Hechingen and Kleinengstingen then two trips between Kleinengstingen and Neufra before returning to Hettington. The 24 Km trip takes 1 hour and includes six stops.

Route 6: Eyach-Haigerloch-Hedhingen. Three trips a day are made over this route on one day of each month during May, July, August and September. With eight stops, the 28 Km long trip takes just over 1 hour.

The fares for all of the above trips are based on the kilometers traveled, which is why the distances haven't been converted to miles. The first number in the price category represents the one-way fare, the second, the round trip fare. 1-12 Km, 5/8 DM; 13-28 Km, 8/12 DM; 29-36 Km, 10/15 DM; 37-44 Km, 12/18 DM; 45-52 Km, 14/20 DM. Children 4 to 14, travel at half the adult fare and there is a "family plan" for up to four persons at a good saving.

Route 7: Still another train makes the trip between Ebingen and Onstmettingen via Tailfingen. This one has the shortest route of the lot, being only 8 Km long and taking but a half-hour, including seven stops. It makes five trips on each of the days it runs, but it runs only two days a year, usually in June.

The fares for this one are 4/6 DM. Children go for half fare and the "family plan" fares are 10/15 DM.

Bicycles, wheel chairs, back packs and even dogs can accompany the rider at no extra cost. This applies to all trains operated by the (EFZ).

Due to the changing nature of the schedule from year to year, actual dates have not been included. For additional information or current schedules, write: Eisenbahnfreunde **Zollernbahn** e. V. (EFZ), Postfach 1168, D-7460 Balingen 1, Germany.

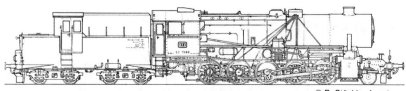

© R. Stöckle, Augsburg

KAISERSTUHL-DAMPFZUG "REBENBUMMLER"

Not far from Freiburg, between the Black Forest and the Rhein River, is a small mountain of volcanic origin known as the Kaiserstuhl. Climatically, the area is one of the warmest in Germany, and, because of the rich volcanic soil, orchards and vineyards thrive there.

Circumventing the Kaiserstuhl is the standard gauge Kaiserstuhlbahn-Gottenheim-Riegel-Breisach Railway, a private, 24-mile long line. The railway came into existence in 1894 as the Kaiserstuhlbahn and was still operating until sometime in the 1970's. The 15.6 mile section of the route between Riegel and Breisach was taken over by the Eisenbahnfreunde Breisgau e. V., which now operates the museum steam train known as the "Rebenbummler" (vineyard stroller). The train literally connects several beautiful old villages as it "strolls" through the scenic wine country. More than a dozen local wines are available from the bar-car during the one hour and twenty minute trip. Eight intermediate stops along the route provide many opportunities for taking pictures.

The train consists of locomotive # 384 (an eight wheeler built by Henschel in 1927) and several 3rd class passenger coaches dating from 1905 to 1928. All of the rolling stock is from the original Kaiserstuhl or neighboring lines, making it one of the few true-to-style local trains still running on its ancient line.

Service is generally on the third Sunday of June, July, August, September and October. Departure time from Reigel is 1030, with arrival in Breisach at 1152. The return trip from Breisach begins at 1625, with the train arriving back in Reigel at 1739. Adult fares are as follows: One-way, 11.- DM; round trip, 18.-DM; half-way from either end, 6.- DM; Children (4-14) go at a reduced rate. Bicycles, motorcycles and backpacks can be carried along free of charge.

In addition, the train can also be chartered for special trips, such things as wine tasting, photography, or just sightseeing.

For additional information, write: Eisenbahnfreunde Breisgau e.V., Eschholzstrasse 40, 7800 Freiburg, Germany.

MUSEUMBAHN WUTACHTAL

For one of the most attractive steam train rides you will find anywhere, try the Museumbahn

A "special train" of the Warthausen-Ochsenhausen line using two of the railway's several steam locomotives. With advance reservations, special trips can be arranged for any time of the year. (Eisenbahn Kurier)

Shown below is engine #7 (TAG 7) of the Tegernseebahn climbing a moderate grade near the town of Gmund. The 1936 vintage Krauss-Maffie engine is most likely hauling a special Christmas train. (Albrecht Sappel, Bayerischer Localbahn Verein e. V.)

Wutachtal in southern Germany. The train runs from Blumberg to Weizen, nearly touching the Swiss border at one point of the 15.6 mile long route. Blumberg is located on highway E27, about half-way between the towns of Schaffhausen and Donaueschingen.

The route takes you through the magnificient Wutachtal River valley over a route that twists and turns like a serpent. Although the direct distance separating the two points is only six miles, plus the altitude difference of 760 feet, it takes approximately 16 miles to cover that distance. If there is a straight stretch of track on the entire trip, it isn't noticable. There are short tunnels, long tunnels and even circular tunnels. In-between the tunnels, there are at least a half dozen viaducts of various lengths and heights. The wild beauty of the Wutachtal valley is well known and there is no better way to enjoy it than by train.

The one hour and ten minute trip to Weizen is all down hill, Weizen being 760 feet lower than the starting point in Blumberg. Although the return trip is all up hill, it takes the same amount of time. Stops are made at five villages along the route: Epfenhofen at (3 miles); Wutachblick (5.4); Futzen (7.8); Grimmelshofen (10.8); Lausheim-Blumegg (13.2); and finally Weizen at 15.6 miles. There is a 50 minute layover at Weizen, which is ample time for a little sightseeing and even something to eat or drink. There is generally a restaurant car on the train but there is so much to see you may prefer not to use your time for dining.

The Museumbahn Wutachtal begins operation at the end of May and continues until the end of September. Service is on most every Saturday and Sunday, with occasional Wednesday and Friday trips added. On some days it makes only one trip, in which case it is always in the afternoon, leaving Blumberg at 1400 and returning at 1700. On all of the other operating days, there are two trips, the first one leaving at 1015 and the second at 1400.

The round trip fares are: 17 DM for adults; 8.50 DM for children (4-14); and free for children under 4 years of age. There is a slight price reduction for groups of 30 or more persons. The schedule for this line is #736 in the Kursbuch.

For more information, write: Stadt Blumberg-Verkehrsamt, 7712 Blumberg 1, Germany.

The Regentalbahn on the Gotteszell blaibach route as it leaves Viechtach. The scenic 24-mile trip through the beautiful Regen valley offers many opportunities for taking photographs. (Morneburg, Bayeischer Localbahn Verein e. V.)

One hundred years old in 1987, the Chiemseebahn's ancient locomotive is still in daily use during the summer months. (Fritz Witzig, Chiemsee Schiffahrt Ludwig-Fessler)

MUSEUMBAHN OCHSENHAUSEN-WARTHAUSEN

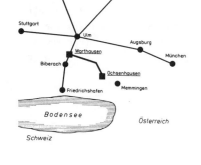

Between Ulm and Lake Constance, there is a narrow gauge (750mm) steam line connecting the towns of Ochsenhausen and Warthausen. Now operated by the Eisenbahn-Kurier Verlag GmbH, the Museumsbahn Ochsenhausen-Warthausen was the last narrow gauge line in active service for the DB.

It was started in 1899 by the Royal Wurttemberg Railways and was operated by them until 1920, when it became part of the Deutsche Reichsbahn. From 1949 until 1983 it served under the banner of the DB. Passenger service on the line ended in 1964, followed by the discontinuance of freight service in 1983, at which time the line was abandoned. It was saved from extinction when, in 1985, it was taken over by the GmbH and made a private museum railway.

The route, which is approximately 11.5 miles long, passes through some beautiful pastoral countryside and is surrounded by lush forests. The trip takes 70 minutes each way and includes stops at five small towns. Maselheim, situated about midway on the route, has a recorded history that goes back 750 years.

The trains operate from May 1 to mid-october, but special trains can be arranged all-year-round. Departure from Ochsenhausen, is every Sunday at 1400 and on Fridays and Saturdays at 0900, 1330 and 1630. Departure from Warthausen is at 1530 on Sundays and at 1030, 1500 and 1800, on Fridays and Saturdays. Fares: adult round trip, 14 DM, one way 10 DM; Children round trip 7 DM, one way 5 DM. Tickets for a portion of the trip can also be purchased. The schedule for this line is number 754 in the DB Kursbuch.

The line's rolling stock consists of: 8 steam locomotives (4 in working condition); 2 diesel locomotives; 2 rail cars; 13 passenger coaches; and 10 freight cars. One of the steam engines is an original 0-4-4-0 Mallet locomotive built in 1899. The trains generally carry up to 300 passengers in five or six vintage carriages, some with open vestibules.

For additional information, write: Eisenbahn Kurier, Mercystrasse 15, Freiburg, Germany.

BAYERISCHER LOCALBAHN VEREIN e. V.

The **Bayerischer Localbahn** Verein operates steam trains over three different routes in the southeastern corner of Germany. Two of the routes are located in the Bayerische region near the Czechoslovakian border and operate as the Regentalbahn AG (RAG). The third route, The Tegernsee-Bahn AG (TAG), lies south of Munich and close to the Austrian border.

From Gotteszell, the Regentalbahn travels northward through the Regen Valley to the town of Blaibach, a distance of 24 miles. As you travel through the beautiful valley, stops are made at Ruhmannsfelden, Teisnach, Gumpenried, Viechtach and Fichtental.

The second route of the Regenbahn begins at Kotzting and goes eastward for 10.6 miles, to the town of Lam. Ten intermediate stops are made during the 38 minute trip, which takes you to within 6 miles of the Czechoslovakian border. Kotzting lies just east of Blaibach.

The route Gotteszell/Viechtach, of the present day Regentalbahn, is descended from the "Lokalbahn Ag Gotteszell-Viechtach," which came into existence in 1890. Since 1891, the remainder of the route, Viechtach/Blaibach, has been part of the "Lokalbahn Deggendorf-Metten AG in Deggendorf."

The route Lam-Kozting, became part of the Regentalbahn in 1973 as a result of a union with the "Lokalbahn AG Lam-Kozting," which founded the line in 1893.

The forerunner of the Tegernsee-Bahn was the "Eisenbahn-Aktiengesellschaft Schaftlach-Gmund am Tegernsee," which was organized in 1883. In the beginning, the Tegernsee-Bahn ran only between Schaftlach and Gmund; the section Gmund-Tegernsee was not added until 1902. In 1942, the line's name was changed to the Tegernsee-Bahn AG.

Today the 7.2 mile route of the Tegernsee-Bahn still connects the towns of Schaftlach and Tegernsee via Gmund and Moosrain.

The rolling stock of the two lines is very extensive. The Regentalbahn alone has in running condition: 14 steam locomotives; 6 diesel locomotives; 11 diesel railcars; and numerous passenger cars.

Added to this is the rolling stock of the Tegernsee-Bahn consisting of the following equipment: 8 steam locomotives; 2 diesel locomotives; 4 diesel railcars; and several passenger coaches.

The steam engines date from 1901 to 1980, with the 1920's, 1950's and 1960's well represented.

Steam trains on the Lam-Kotzting route generally run on the second and third Sundays of June, July, August and September. Departures from Lam are at 0945, 1330 and 1520. Arrival in Kotzting is at 1023, 1408 and 1558. The first train departs Kotzting for Lam at 1145. Fares are: Adult round trip, 10 DM; Children round trip, 5 DM. All-day passes can be purchased for 20 DM and 10 DM, respectively.

Operating days for the Blaibach-Viechtach-Gotteszell trip are the first and last Sundays of June, July and August. The first of two trains departs Blaibach at 0950, arriving in Gotteszell at 1135. The second train leaves at 1740, but it goes only as far as Viechtach. There is also a second train from Viechtach that leaves for Gotteszell at 1435. Fares for the round trip are: Adults, 14 DM; children, 7 DM. All-day passes are 20 DM and 10 DM.

The Tegernsee-Bahn also operates only on Sundays, usually the first and third. An extra Sunday trip is sometimes added during August and September, however. Round trip fares are: Adults, 8 DM; children, 4 DM. All-day passes are 12 DM and 6 DM.

Next to the old (1877) railway station in Bayerische Eisenstein, about 15 miles southeast of Lam, is the Bayerische Eisenstein Lokalbahn Museum. A large collection of historic steam engines, coaches and other memorabilia of the Regental-bahn and the Tegernsee-Bahn are located there.

CHIEMSEE-BAHN

Just north of the Bernau exit off the Munich/Salzburg Autobahn is the lakeside town of Prien.

During the summer months, the steam-powered Chiemsee-Bahn carries passengers between the station in Prien and the port, a distance of just over one mile. Pulled by an 1887 steam locomotive, the train, with its five or six old-time cars carrying up to 350 persons, makes the trip in about 10 minutes. Departure is more or less hourly all day and the fare is a mere 1.50 DM or 2.50 DM round trip.

The little railway, which celebrated its 100th birthday on July 10 1987, carries up to 100,000 passengers each year.

For additional information, write: Chiemsee-Schiffahrt, Ludwig Fessler, D-821 Prien a.Ch. Postfach 21, Germany.

ABOUT THE AUTHOR

Unlike most writers of train books, Mr. Winn's railroad experience, except for a very brief stint at Southern Pacific, is limited mainly to train travel.

Bernard's interest in rail-roads goes back to the early 1930's, however, when, at age 14, he bought his first electric train set. At age 17, with his friend Paul, he hopped his first "freight" out of Oakland, California and spent the next two months riding the rails. Bumming meals, eating in railroad jungles, and sleeping wherever there was shelter, he traveled across the country as an uninvited guest of the railroads. By the time Bernard had completed two more summers as a "Gentleman of the Road," he was hooked on "railroading," a term generally reserved for train crewmen.

Bernard's train travel has not all been via a "side door Pullman," however. During six month-long trips in the past ten years, Bernard and his wife, Audrey, have traveled extensively by train in nearly every European Country. The last two trips were devoted almost entirely to research for this and other books to follow.

This is the second book written and published by Bernard Winn. "Getting High in Europe," a guide to high places in Europe, was released in 1985 and is still in print.

Book Ordering   Information

GETTING HIGH IN EUROPE; a guide to high places in 218 European Cities.   A spiral-bound, pocket size book of 150 pages plus illustrations. $5.95

RAILWAYS REVISITED, a guide to little-known railways in AUSTRIA and GERMANY. A profusely illustrated 8-1/2 x 11 paperback, $8.95.

Both books are available from Incline Press, 456 Columbia Ave. P.O.Box 212, Merced, CA 95341. The price, which includes postage, handling, and tax where applicable, must accompany all orders.